Praise for The Restored Organization

"The Restored Organization is all about leading with heart and vision. It offers practical advice and real-world strategies to help you build a culture that supports well-being, encourages accountability, and fosters continuous growth. If you're looking to create a workplace where people thrive, this book is your guide."

– Piyush Gupta, CEO, DBS Bank, Singapore

"The Restored Organization is your ultimate guide to thriving in the digital age. It challenges you to rethink your approach and foster a culture of innovation, collaboration, and people-centricity. A must-read for visionary leaders eager to shape the future of work."

– Tian Chong Ng, CEO, Singtel, Singapore

"Bringing about cultural change is the 'hardest of tasks' that demands the 'softest of skills' for leaders. At the heart of it all stands human behavior, still being discovered in the world of AI and acting as transformative glue. The Restored Organization is a must-read book that highlights the vital areas of restoring an organizational culture, before it is too late."

– KV Rao, Chairman, Tata International, Singapore

"A strategic exploration of both personal and organizational leadership strategies, designed to have positive outcomes in an ever-changing landscape. An invigorating read for any leader."

– Ivan Chin, CEO, Extra•Ordinary People, Singapore

"In a culture that often puts performance over people, The Restored Organization reminds us that genuine progress is fuelled by trust, respect, and authenticity. It's the perfect guide for leaders who value the human side of work as much as the bottom line."

– Dr. Anna A. Tavis, Department Chair,
Human Capital Management, New York University

THE RESTORED ORGANIZATION

SIX WAYS TO HUMANIZE WORKPLACE CULTURES AND TRANSFORM RESULTS

NITIN GOIL & SEBASTIAN ANTHONY

ISBN
Paperback 979-8-89777-306-0
Hardcase 979-8-89929-288-0

Dedication

I dedicate this book to my late dad Anil, who always led with humanity. I'm immensely grateful for all the life and business lessons he taught me and for instilling in me values of authenticity, integrity, and empathy. I miss you dad, but I know you'll be proud that I wrote this book.

– Nitin

Contents

Acknowledgments

Nitin Goil

With so much of our time and energy given to work, it can and should be a source of joy. I hope that the research, stories, and structure we've shared in this book help you realize the importance of human-centered workplaces that you all deserve. When Sebastian and I first started talking about this concept more than two years ago, I never imagined both of us collaborating to write this book and, with it, having the chance to help so many organizations create deeper purpose, engagement, and happiness in their workplaces. It truly is a dream come true. Thank you, Sebastian, for your friendship, for your unconditional support, and for partnering with me on this exciting journey.

I'm grateful to many people for their help, first and foremost God, for his continued presence and blessing in my life. A huge thanks to my family, especially my wife Vishikha and my son Viyaan. Your support and encouragement made finishing the book not just possible but also truly enjoyable.

My sincere gratitude to Michael Bush for believing in this book and taking the time to write the foreword. It means a lot to us, Michael, and we appreciate it very much. I'm also incredibly lucky to have worked with two inspiring leaders, Dr. Peggy Crowe and Dr. Roland Smith, who showed me what humanized leadership truly is, and I'm thankful for their support during my challenging times. My deep appreciation also goes to Dr. Aaron Hughey for inspiring me with your teaching and making me fall in love with research and writing.

Very importantly, I'm extremely grateful to all the leaders we interviewed during this process and everyone who took the time to speak to us and share their stories. It was very inspiring for us, and I hope it can be inspirational for you too as you read the book. Lastly, my humble thanks to the NeuroLeadership Institute for giving me the opportunity to learn and apply neuroscience in everything I do, both at work and in my personal life.

Nothing excites me more than knowing that I can play my small part in making a positive impact in humanizing workplaces and helping organizations get fully restored.

Sebastian Anthony

Coming across The Second Mountain by David Brooks some years ago set me on the path of discovering and climbing my own 'Second Mountain.' Little did I know that I would be writing about this journey alongside my good friend Nitin. As we shared our stories and "battle scars," we realized we had the power to make a difference. Instead of just swapping stories, we decided to make our experiences count by impacting lives and equipping leaders to transform their workplaces into better places to work. Thank you, Nitin, for your empathetic ear, friendship, and support.

First and foremost, my gratitude goes to God Almighty for being a "*light unto my feet*" and helping me navigate numerous trials. The lessons learned from these experiences have been invaluable. I'm deeply appreciative of my wife, Grace, for being my pillar of strength during difficult times. Special thanks to David, Joan, and Hannah for their unwavering support and encouragement on social media.

I have been fortunate to encounter many great leaders throughout my life, some of whom are mentioned in this book. The late Maj Surajan was especially inspirational to me. Others who have given me their time and encouragement include John Bittleston, Eliza Quek, and Stephen Krempl.

This book would not have been possible without the personal stories and experiences shared by over 100 leaders over the past two years. You know who you are- thank you all for helping to restore me so that I may now help restore others and enable them to humanize their workplaces.

Foreword

There is one truth that remains constant in today's changing business environment: workplace culture matters. As we continue to navigate the demands and challenges of a post-pandemic complex world, it has never been more critical to create a positive, inclusive, and empowering workplace culture. "The Restored Organization" offers invaluable insights into core issues and opportunities for organizations to humanize their workplace cultures and transform financial results.

As the CEO of a Great Place to Work™, I have the chance to see firsthand how strong, healthy high-trust workplace cultures transform the employee experience and ultimately, the business. Great workplaces have trust built in at their core. At the opposite end of the spectrum are toxic environments that have eroded all trust and stifle the organization's journey toward greatness. These workplaces are a great place to work for some, not all.

"The Restored Organization" gives a compelling framework for organizations wanting to humanize their workplaces and create thriving, high performing cultures. Based on the author's own experiences and informed by their interviews with over 100 leaders in Asia and globally, this book presents a fresh take on toxic cultures and how to create an environment where both people and results can thrive.

At the core of this book is the innovative FLOWER Framework™, which provides a holistic approach and a roadmap for organizations to relook and assess their workplace culture. The framework's six "petals" - Fulfilling Culture, Listening Culture, Ownership Culture, Well-being Culture, Enterprising Culture, and Results-based Culture - align with principles we also champion at Great Place To Work™.

Through a Fulfilling Culture, organizations can create purpose and meaning in work. In today's age, employees do not seek only monetary compensation for their work but also want to know that what they're doing contributes toward something bigger. That resonates very well with our own research findings: In over 170 countries, organizations that provide a sense of purpose outperform others in many ways related to employee engagement and retention. This is especially brought to light through the emphasis on a Listening Culture.

An organization can only harness the full potential of its diversified workforce by building trust and ensuring that every voice is heard. Not only does this approach enhance innovation, but it creates a sense of belonging that is very important in building a great workplace. When people know that their leader cares about them as a person, not just an employee, there is trust, and they feel motivated and empowered.

The focus on Well-being Culture is timely and equally important. As the lines blur between work and personal life today, taking care of health, work-life balance, and general wellness of employees becomes non-negotiable. When this is positive, employees are four times more likely to stay, two times more likely to be proud of their accomplishments, and three times more likely to endorse their company and its products and services to friends and family.

Perhaps the greatest value this book adds is that of a pragmatic approach. The ability to mesh insights from research and neuroscience with many real-life examples and bite-sized micro case studies makes "The Restored Organization" eminently practical. This blending of theory and application is very critical in the heightened pace of change within any organization.

As a professional dedicated to helping organizations create a Great Place to Work For All™, I found the holistic view of organizational culture in this book very enlightening. The authors correctly note that a thriving culture is not based on one thing but how all these components play together. Leaders can build a strong cultural ecosystem for the success of individuals and organizations alike by focusing on fulfillment, listening, ownership, well-being, enterprise, and results.

"The Restored Organization" is at the same time both a resource and an urgent call to action. It calls upon us to remember that positive workplace culture building is never a one-time act; it is something continuous.

Continuing attentiveness, the courage for continuous self-reflection, and readiness for continuous change. Looking from the future of work perspective, the organizations that will really thrive in the future will have culture as an integral part of their strategy- a powerful enabler that fosters innovation, productivity, and ultimately, leads to sustained success.

This book is a timely and important read for leaders, HR professionals, and anyone interested in creating a healthier, more engaged, and productive work environment. It challenges us to critically examine our organizations and take concrete steps toward building cultures that empower and support people.

As we design the future of work, "The Restored Organization" serves as both a guide and inspiration. By embracing its principles and strategies, leaders can create workplaces built on respect, empathy, and understanding - benefiting both the workforce and the bottom line.

This is why I believe the future of work is for all.

– **Michael Bush**
CEO, Great Place To Work™

Preface

We want to start this journey with you by sharing something personal- a conversation, if you will, about why this book came to be. It all begins with a question we've asked ourselves countless times: Why did we feel so compelled to write this? The answer lies in our own experiences, stories shaped by a phenomenon that has impacted many but is spoken of far less than it should be- working in toxic work cultures.

These moments and memories are etched into who we are and are the starting point of everything that follows in this book. We both experienced firsthand how toxic leaders can create workplaces that erode professional growth and personal well-being. They created environments where stress was the norm, voices were silent, and purpose felt out of reach. Over time, these experiences turned into questions: Why do such cultures persist? How can organizations move beyond them? And most importantly, how can we restore workplaces where people genuinely find meaning at work and are highly performing?

Although it wasn't easy to revisit these memories, our hope is that, by beginning with this personal foundation, we can invite you into a larger conversation – one about possibility and restoration. We have included real-life experiences, including our own, of dealing with dysfunctional and toxic work environments. To respect the sensitivity of some of these stories, we have changed names and, in a few cases, adjusted identifying details. This applies to both the accounts shared with us and the first-hand experiences we've had. Our intent is to ensure confidentiality while shedding light on the challenges of workplace toxicity in organizations and sharing effective ways to restore cultures.

Nitin Goil

As mentioned in my acknowledgments, I've worked with some great leaders in my career who've role-modeled human-centered leadership. These leaders ensured I felt valued beyond my job title. They gave me autonomy and trusted me to make decisions, and their empathetic leadership style fostered a supportive environment that allowed me to learn and grow in a positive way. On the other hand, I've also worked with leaders who were micromanagers, and they prioritized their ego over team welfare. Working under such leaders felt like navigating a minefield. I didn't know what to expect, and work felt like fighting for survival.

One such experience was when I worked in a global organization that seemed full of promise, and all looked great when I interviewed and even on joining. However, stepping into this new work environment brought its own set of challenges with the career switch that I had made consciously. While I had hoped to ease into the role with guidance and camaraderie, I often felt isolated and unsure of navigating the new ways of working.

Despite my growing insecurities, I displayed a confident front, learning as much as I could, determined to prove my capabilities. My boss, Jamie, had high expectations and assumed I could hit the ground running without much support. She often asked for updates or had me join client calls, expecting I would know everything immediately. I leaned on her for direction, hoping for the guidance I desperately needed but never got. But no matter how much I learned and the effort I put in, it never seemed to be enough in her eyes. Slowly, I began to realize that her expectations were impossible to meet, and her dissatisfaction was becoming personal. She would tear into my performance, questioning my qualifications, and launching into personal attacks. Her words were not constructive; they were meant to hurt.

The dread didn't stay confined to the office. It followed me home, turning evenings and weekends into stretches of anxiety. Jamie's calls during off-hours became a constant source of fear. They weren't about support or collaboration; they were about pointing out flaws and belittling me further. The toll on my mental health was staggering. Tasks I once approached with confidence now felt insurmountable. I doubted my every move, constantly worrying about making mistakes and enduring more confrontations. Sleepless nights became my new normal, and the stress began to manifest physically- tightness in my chest, a racing heart, and moments where I felt on the verge of breaking down completely. My self-esteem, once a solid foundation, had crumbled terribly.

Leaving that environment was a relief, but the scars remain. The self-doubt, anxiety, and lingering sense of inadequacy still resurface at times. In the aftermath of it all, I found a source of strength in my conversations with a close friend and ex-colleague, Sebastian Anthony. Sebastian was a lifeline, offering a judgment-free space to share my experiences. Together, we realized that we both went through similar experiences, and it uncovered the stark reality that our stories were not unique and toxic work cultures were everywhere, affecting countless others like us.

Those conversations sparked something bigger than just shared frustrations. They planted the seed for systemic change – a desire to challenge pervasive norms in organizations and find ways to create workplaces built on respect, empathy, and integrity. This shared purpose became the foundation of this book, a journey toward humanizing workplaces where everyone can thrive to achieve results.

Sebastian Anthony

I have worked in organizations that were led by visionary, energized, highly engaged leaders, or as I would call it, an "abundance mentality." I have also worked under leaders who embraced the concept of a "scarcity mentality," where they focused mainly on pushing their own agendas or putting members of their team down to boost their own prestige or ego.

I once worked as an Organizational Development Consultant in an organization where my role was to reshape the culture and create openness and transparency. The work was demanding, and it wasn't an easy task. As an individual contributor, I juggled many responsibilities, and it required a constant balancing act. Thankfully, I wasn't doing it alone. Certain departments and colleagues proved to be invaluable collaborators. Together, we navigated the complexities of the role, supporting each other as we worked toward creating an environment where change felt possible.

A new supervisor, Jim, was brought on board to oversee several functions including mine. At first, it all seemed fine until he began questioning and scrutinizing my team members, to the point of embarrassing them, and it led to some of them quitting. Jim would often say that they are not good enough to justify his actions. But only when he started picking on me did I realize the level of his viciousness. At first, it was subtle- small remarks here and there, and at times, sarcastic. But it quickly escalated. Every decision I made seemed to invite scrutiny, and his micromanagement grew relentless. He would ask me to explain the rationale behind even the smallest decisions, often in a way that felt more like an interrogation than collaboration. His sarcasm during meetings became particularly grating, with comments designed to undermine me in front of others.

And then came what I started referring to as the "20 questions" ordeal. Whenever I sent him an email for approval or feedback, he would respond with an overwhelming number of questions, most of which seemed unnecessary and overly detailed. Answering them consumed an extraordinary amount of time, pulling me away from other important tasks. If I didn't respond quickly enough, he accused me of stalling or being unprepared. And if I did respond thoroughly, the process would start all over again with another round of questions. It was exhausting and demoralizing, a never-ending cycle that kept me on edge and made even the simplest tasks feel insurmountable.

A good number of us who have spent enough time in organizations can empathize with situations like this, where you start questioning your own self-worth after being subjected to this kind of "psychological abuse."

It was around this time that a friend introduced me to The Second Mountain by David Brooks, a book that explores the idea of finding deeper purpose and fulfillment beyond the surface successes of life. Inspired by this thought, I engaged in deep conversations with Nitin Goil, another good friend and former colleague, who also faced similar challenges. As we spoke, we realized that we were not alone, as both of us, in the course of our work, met hundreds of people yearly, many of whom also shared similar experiences.

We both decided to work together to channel this negative energy into something positive and purposeful. This pursuit led us to "The Restored Organization", a concept rooted in two fundamental questions: what if the harm caused by workplace toxic environments could be undone? And what if organizations could be transformed into spaces where people could truly thrive and still deliver exceptional results?

We explored the foundation of restoring an organization's culture, starting with leadership and evolving into something larger – a vision for restoring entire organizations. Along the way, we tried and tested different approaches, drawing from our own experiences, those of others, and the insights we gained through reflection.

What unfolded during this process is at the heart of the book you're holding now. We realize there are a lot of self-help and leadership books out there on this topic, but none examine restoration from a systems perspective- one that considers the organization's culture as a whole. This book goes beyond individual leadership advice and is designed to help leaders, teams, and organizations focus on systemic changes that can help restore their workplace cultures fully. The outlined approach we share is very comprehensive and contains strategies, best practices, and micro case studies of organizations globally that have successfully done this.

In the pages ahead, we'll take you through a structure that became central to this vision- the FLOWER Framework™. Our exploration begins with an unflinching look at the problem- the pervasive nature of toxic workplace cultures around the world and their profound impact. These cultures thrive in silence and indifference, often hidden beneath layers of routine and norms, yet their consequences are anything but invisible. Recognizing this harsh reality lays the groundwork for understanding the urgent need for change.

From this recognition, we transition to the path of restoration, examining its implications at the individual, team, and organizational levels. Change, as we've learned through our journey, must begin from the ground up. It requires addressing the very roots of an organization's culture rather than masking symptoms with temporary fixes. This is where the framework comes in to serve as the guide for this restoration process. It offers a way to restore organizations by focusing on actionable steps that address the core of the problem while ensuring trust, empathy, and innovation.

The framework itself is explored in depth, with each chapter diving into distinct subcultures essential for cultural restoration. Within each subculture, we examine its three key elements, providing three actionable strategies to cultivate these elements in an organization. Each part of this discourse is intentional and interconnected, just as the pieces of a healthy organizational culture must be. The toxic cultures we examine in the beginning connect directly to the pressing need for restoration, which flows naturally into the structured path charted by the framework. The framework itself is not a collection of isolated ideas; its elements are deeply intertwined, designed to work together to create a thriving and sustainable workplace. In these pages, you'll see how this interconnectedness mirrors the complexity of organizational culture and the importance of addressing it holistically.

There is deliberate thought behind why we chose to focus on only three elements and strategies for each subculture. This is rooted in how our brains are wired to process and retain information. The "Power of Three" is a concept deeply embedded in cognitive neuroscience and psychology, and it underscores the brain's natural preference for triads. This structure is powerful, tapping into how we think, learn, and make sense of the world. Our working memory, which holds and processes information temporarily, plays a central role in this. Research shows that working memory is limited in capacity, optimally handling three to four chunks of information at a time. This insight aligns with the findings of George Miller's foundational research on cognitive limits, later refined to emphasize three as an ideal number for effective processing. Neuroscientific studies show that regions like the prefrontal cortex, essential for working memory tasks, are most efficient when managing smaller, well-structured sets of information.

By structuring the elements of the framework around three elements, along with their respective strategies, we've ensured that this book presents ideas in a way that aligns with your brain's natural strengths. Every choice, every structure, is intentional. It's about making the path to restoration practical and effective.

Throughout this journey, we will keep revisiting neuroscience and psychology to uncover the "why" behind the importance of each element. At the same time, we know that science and theory need to be anchored in real-life. Hence, each chapter includes real-life examples of leaders and organizations who have excelled in this area and have been recognized by entities like Great Place To Work™. Alongside these, we've included moments from our own experiences, sometimes painful, sometimes hopeful- because we know that shared stories can bridge understanding in ways that theory cannot. These examples bring credibility to the principles we outline, grounding them in the reality of organizational life and making them tangible for you. To deepen this connection, each chapter includes detailed micro case studies that explore the elements within the framework, offering a closer look at their practical implications and the results they can yield when applied thoughtfully.

Additionally, you'll find reflections at the end of each chapter with questions designed to guide you toward introspection and self-evaluation and help you consider steps you can take toward building something better and restoring your own workplace fully.

Introduction

We've all heard the old phrase *"Culture eats strategy for breakfast"* by Peter Drucker. It is still true today, and culture still plays a very critical role in organizational success. However, in 2020, when the world was in the throes of the pandemic, the scrutiny of culture began. Everything changed in an instant. Offices, once buzzing with energy, fell silent. Desks sat abandoned, and the vibrant rhythm of workplace life came to an abrupt halt. Employees who had once thrived on face-to-face meetings and daily commutes now found themselves adapting to home offices, trying to balance work amidst the unpredictability of life.

The change came swiftly, leaving little room for anyone to fully prepare or process what was happening. Supply chains were interrupted, industries faced unprecedented challenges, and the way we worked completely flipped. For the first time, organizations were forced to acknowledge that their traditional ways of operating could no longer work with this new wave of disruption. Almost overnight, companies pivoted to adopt digital tools. Video calls became the new norm, and online platforms became the core of daily operations. Remote work, which had previously been an option for a select few, was now the standard.

As companies settled into this new normal, it quickly became clear that the rapid changes had left many organizations struggling to maintain a sense of stability. The shift to remote work, combined with the rush to embrace digital tools, often resulted in fragmented communication. People who were once used to the groove of office life suddenly felt isolated. Teams, once working together in close quarters, found themselves scattered, trying to keep up with the changing dynamics of their roles. This created a growing sense of anxiety and uncertainty. Employees were left wondering where they stood within their organizations and what the future holds for them.

Around the globe, companies were on the hunt for a strategy that could help bring back some sort of clarity. Leaders were focused on immediate solutions – keeping operations running, managing remote teams, and somehow surviving. But amidst all the chaos, something became clear. The answer wasn't just in the newest technology or the most efficient processes. It was something that had been sidelined for years, often considered "soft" or less urgent. That something was culture.

Culture was the foundation that had quietly been holding everything together all these years. It was a significant piece that could bring people together and create a sense of belonging in an uncertain world. But why was this so important?

In times of crisis, everything in an organization can feel very unclear. The usual routines break down, and people start to feel lost. That's when a strong sense of culture becomes essential. It's what gives people a sense of direction and helps them feel connected, even when everything else is uncertain.

Aaron Antonovsky's concept of Sense of Coherence (SOC) gives us a way to understand this better. SOC revolves around three essential ideas: comprehensibility, manageability, and meaningfulness. Comprehensibility is about making things clear. At the workplace, people want clarity on what's happening around them, and this comes from clear communication and consistent leadership. When the culture emphasizes transparency, employees know what's expected, and the unpredictability that often leads to stress is reduced. They aren't left guessing about changes or direction; instead, they feel informed and involved in the process.

Next is manageability. A culture that provides the right direction and support creates a sense of confidence in employees. They feel ready to meet the challenges because the environment gives them the resources and guidance they need. In this type of culture, employees aren't overwhelmed because they have what they need to succeed.

Finally, meaningfulness ties everything together. People need to feel that their work has value and purpose. When the culture highlights how each role connects to a larger goal, employees become more engaged and resilient. They see the significance of what they do, and that sense of purpose drives them, even in tough times.

Organizations are no different from individuals in this regard. Companies that create a culture built around the principles of coherence, such as clarity, support, and purpose, are far better equipped to handle uncertainty. During the pandemic, companies with a strong sense of coherence maintained high employee morale and engagement because their culture helped employees understand the situation better, effectively manage new challenges, and stay connected through meaningful work.

As the importance of culture becomes more evident in ensuring a Sense of Coherence, it also evolves into something deeper. One aspect of this evolution is the psychological contract, which refers to the unspoken agreements between employers and employees. It's not something you'll find in a formal job offer, but it's felt in every interaction and expectation. This contract is crucial because it shapes how employees view their roles, their relationship with their employer, and, ultimately, their place within the organization.

Historically, the psychological contract was simple, focusing on job security and a steady paycheck. But times have changed and so have people's needs. Employees are no longer content with just financial rewards; they are looking for a work environment that reflects their personal values and adapts to their life circumstances. This shift in priorities is reflected in the new elements that have become part of the psychological contract now-flexibility, empathy, and inclusion.

One of the clearest shifts is in the demand for flexibility. The pandemic proved that remote work can be productive, and for many, even improve work-life balance. As a result, employees now expect more autonomy and control over their schedules and work environments. They want to manage their time in ways that suit their personal and professional lives.

As flexibility became a central expectation in the evolving psychological contract, so did the need for empathy. Leaders who can truly connect with their teams, show compassion and care for their well-being, are much better positioned to create a supportive environment where trust flourishes. This kind of leadership makes people feel valued and helps build loyalty. When employees believe their leaders are genuinely invested in them, they are far more likely to remain engaged, even in the face of challenges.

In addition to flexibility and empathy, there's also been a growing focus on inclusion within the psychological contract. Employees now expect their organizations to go beyond token gestures of representation. They want to see real action toward creating an environment where everyone feels included and respected, regardless of their background or identity. It's about making sure that all voices are heard and valued.

As the importance and the role of organizational culture deepens, we must ponder a critical question:

Are organizations truly adapting to this new understanding? Are they evolving fast enough to keep up with the emerging needs of their employees?

For many organizations, the answer isn't so clear. In today's world, shaped by constant volatility and uncertainty, businesses are being pulled in different directions, with a high level of expectations from various stakeholders and customers. The urgency of stabilizing supply chains, accelerating digital transformation, and the focus on business results comes with a culture compromise- organizations have less time to focus on employee engagement and the well-being of their employees.

The effects of this cultural compromise became evident in the wake of the Great Resignation, a significant economic trend that began in early 2021 during the COVID-19 pandemic, where millions of workers voluntarily left their jobs in search of better pay, improved working conditions, or more fulfilling roles. An October 2021 Harvard Business Review report highlighted that 55% of workers planned to leave their jobs within a year, citing disengagement and a lack of connection as key reasons. At the height of the Great Resignation in 2022, over 50 million Americans quit their jobs, averaging nearly 4.5 million resignations per month.

As organizations continue to adjust to this changing world and strive to retain their talent, they will need to recalibrate how they operate. This recalibration presents an opportunity to rebuild and redefine cultures in ways that haven't been done before. Organizations will need to find the right balance between being human-centric and result-oriented, and failing to do so, they will be confronted with a harsh reality: employee disengagement, erosion of trust, and a toxic workplace culture.

The Effects of Toxicity

In every corner of the world, regardless of industry or size, organizations are grappling with this pervasive issue of toxicity. In the past, when people heard the phrase "toxic work environment," they often thought about physical dangers at work. The safety warnings and hazard signs were a constant reminder of them. But now, the term has morphed into a metaphor for something far less visible yet equally dangerous. It's not about the risks that are visually seen but those that aren't seen: the undermining managers, the corrosive office politics, the relentless pressure without support.

Toxicity in the workplace can take many forms. It can be the manager who belittles their team, the lack of clear communication or direction, or even the tension between coworkers that festers over time. These environments often breed bullying, harassment, exclusion, and unethical behavior, creating a high-stress environment where dissatisfaction becomes the norm.

The impact of toxic cultures is undeniable. A 2024 report by American job site Monster says nearly 7 in 10 workers (67%) feel they work in a toxic environment (+4% from 2023), and roughly three-quarters (74%) say their mental health at work is poor, with 62% saying a toxic work culture is to blame. That's millions of people working in environments that chip away their health, morale, and overall happiness.

In Singapore, the situation is equally concerning. According to a report by the ADP Research Institute titled "People at Work 2023: A Global Workforce View", 68% of employees reported experiencing stress at work. Many of these employees felt unsupported by their employers. The report highlighted that, despite the increased focus on mental health during the pandemic, support systems have diminished as organizations prioritize growth again, leaving employees struggling to cope with ongoing stress without adequate resources or assistance.

The truth is that even organizations celebrated for their high standards and innovation aren't immune to the dangers of toxic workplace cultures. In fact, some of the most successful organizations have faced harsh criticism of the way they treat their employees. Amazon is a clear example. While the organization is known for its operational excellence and ability to deliver almost anything to your doorstep in record time, many employees describe a very different reality behind the scenes.

Amazon's work environment has been reportedly called a pressure cooker, where employees face relentless demands and expectations that can feel impossible to meet. This constant push for productivity comes at a cost. In January 2023, a survey by UNI Global Union, which included over 2,000 Amazon workers from eight different countries, found that more than half felt their physical health was suffering due to the organization's intense monitoring of performance. What was even more troubling was that 57% of these workers reported that their mental health had been negatively impacted as well.

But these numbers don't tell the whole story. When you dig deeper into employee experiences, you find reports of burnout, high turnover, and a general feeling of being trapped in a bureaucratic system that crushes morale.

The challenges seen at Amazon are, unfortunately, not confined to one organization. Another example comes from Razer, a leading gaming hardware organization based in Singapore, where similar issues have been reported. In 2019, concerns emerged about the intense atmosphere within the company, largely driven by the leadership style of co-founder Tan Min-Liang. Employees described a culture where verbal abuse was commonplace, and dismissals were frequent, often for minor infractions. While the organization focused on performance-fueled innovation, it left many employees feeling more oppressed than motivated. The high-demanding environment created significant stress and dissatisfaction, with job security always in question, causing employees to struggle under the weight of ever-increasing demands.

These stories show that toxic cultures aren't limited to specific industries or regions. They're a global problem, affecting organizations of all sizes, even those with the highest standards and most innovative products. And so, it begs the question: How do so many organizations let toxic cultures go unchecked?

A key factor is leadership. Leaders play a crucial role in shaping an organization's culture by setting expectations and modeling behaviors. If leaders lead by putting pressure to succeed at any cost, they tend to display cut-throat behaviors where success is measured only by performance metrics and short-term gains. When they prioritize these metrics over the well-being of their employees, it creates a fertile ground for toxicity to flourish.

Johnny C. Taylor Jr., President and CEO of the Society for Human Resource Management (SHRM), notes that *"cut-throat culture can even exist in nonprofits."* He points out that it's ultimately people-led: *"If management believes in winning by all means, then it becomes the corporate culture."*

In environments where collaboration and ethics are overshadowed by the drive for results, employees may feel forced into a survival mindset. The constant pressure to outperform leads to a breakdown in teamwork, as individuals prioritize personal success. This creates an environment where blame games and office politics flourish, slowly undermining a vital element of human interaction: empathy. In environments where employees feel they must constantly compete for results, communication and connection between leaders and their teams begin to fade.

This shift doesn't happen overnight, but once it takes root, the effects are clear. Leaders and managers, often overwhelmed by the need to hit targets, become less attuned to the personal and psychological needs of their workforce. The focus on numbers and performance leaves little room for addressing the emotional well-being of employees.

When you consider all these factors and when the right leaders are not in place, the workplace becomes a place of dread and toxicity thrives. And the costs, both human and financial, can become alarmingly high for organizations.

Why Toxicity is Everyone's Problem

On a seemingly ordinary day in 2024, the tragic story of Anna Sebastian Perayil, a 26-year-old chartered accountant at Ernst & Young (EY) in Pune, India, shook the corporate world. Anna, just four months into her job, tragically passed away from cardiac arrest.

Anna's mother, Anita Augustine, shared a deeply emotional letter following her daughter's death, addressed to Rajiv Memani, the Chairman of EY India. In her letter, she blamed the relentless workload for driving her daughter to physical and emotional exhaustion, which tragically resulted in her untimely passing. The letter went viral, gaining traction on social media and inspiring others to share their own stories of struggling within toxic workplaces, amplifying a message that this problem affects countless lives.

Rajiv Memani responded to the outpouring of grief and criticism by offering his condolences and acknowledging the growing concerns about the pressures within EY. He stressed that taking care of employees' well-being is a top priority at EY and they're committed to it. However, he denied that workload played a direct role in Anna's death, explaining that her assignments were comparable to those of her peers. Memani's response, while intended to reassure, underscores a disconnect between corporate leaders and the realities their employees face – a gap that often leads to toxic work cultures.

Considering Anna's story, it becomes clear just how vital it is for everyone within an organization, from top executives to entry-level staff, to actively engage in creating a supportive and safe work culture. It's a crucial step toward ensuring no employee must compromise their mental and physical health for their job. It is a sobering reminder that workplace toxicity, if left unchecked, can lead to devastating losses.

➤ *The Individual Impact*

Anna's experience wasn't an isolated event; it's a reality that many people face, often silently, each day. The emotional toll begins the moment someone wakes up, dreading the thought of going to work. That sinking feeling in the pit of one's stomach, the constant stress, and the fear of making a mistake, all start to pile up.

It's a gradual build up that affects both the mind and body, often without employees fully realizing how much it affects them. This is where our natural stress responses come into play, especially the fight-or-flight mechanism. Our bodies are wired to protect us from danger, and when we feel threatened, the fight-or-flight response kicks in. Centuries ago, when humans went out hunting, always on alert, they scanned their surroundings for any sign of danger. Then, when a predator showed up suddenly, the body reacted, the heart raced, adrenaline kicked in, and the muscles tensed up. The choice became simple: fight the threat or flight - run as fast as you can.

This fight-or-flight response is deeply ingrained in us, a survival mechanism that has helped humans face physical threats for generations. It is driven by the amygdala, the part of the brain that processes emotions and detects danger. When it senses a threat, the amygdala signals the body to release stress hormones like adrenaline and cortisol.

Fast forward to today, and while the office has replaced the wilderness, our body's response to perceived threats remains the same. Instead of facing a wild animal, we now face tight deadlines, difficult coworkers, or a boss who criticizes without offering support. Even though the threat isn't physical, our body reacts as if it is.

This also ties into how our brains are wired to minimize threats and rewards. Neuroscientist Evian Gordon describes this as the brain's core organizing principle. And shares how we react differently to direct versus indirect threats. His research shows that while direct threats might propel us into action to think and act quickly, indirect threats can cause us to freeze or retreat. Imagine being in a workplace where the pressure from a colleague or boss feels like an indirect threat. You might find yourself pulling away, dodging certain tasks, or even steering clear of meetings to escape the discomfort.

Over time, this constant state of discomfort can impair cognitive functions like memory, decision-making, and problem-solving because the brain diverts its resources away from high order thinking to deal with the perceived danger.

If you're always under stress, your amygdala, the alarm bell in your brain, becomes overly sensitive, causing you to react more intensely to everyday situations. This can crank up your anxiety levels and make it harder to shake off the tension, even when you're away from work. This ongoing strain can also pave the way for serious issues like depression and burnout, trapping you in a cycle of stress and heightened vigilance that's tough to break.

➤ *The Team Impact*

Once toxic behaviors and attitudes start affecting individuals, they can spread quickly to teams. It's like throwing a stone into a pond; the ripples may begin on one side but may soon be seen throughout the pond. In the same way, toxicity may start with one person, but its effects may soon pervade across the team environment, fundamentally altering how teams function and how individuals within those teams interact.

At the team level, one of the first things that gets eroded is trust. Trust is essential for any team to thrive and allows team members to communicate openly, share ideas without fear, and rely on one another to get things done. When managers create an environment of fear or suspicion, employees start to feel like they can't depend on their leaders or even their peers. They become more guarded, less willing to share openly, and more focused on protecting themselves than working collaboratively.

This breakdown in trust leads to communication issues. Instead of working together toward common goals, team members might begin to withhold information, avoid difficult conversations, or only speak up when they feel absolutely safe. When communication starts to falter, the ability to collaborate effectively disappears. Teams that were once cohesive and dynamic now break down, stifling innovation and problem-solving.

This can result in increased hostility among team members and make collaborative work impossible. This environment significantly impacts employee engagement and productivity, with disengagement leading to widespread dissatisfaction. In fact, the presence of just one toxic employee can reduce the entire team's performance by up to 40%, as demonstrated by Felps, Mitchell, and Byington in their 2006 study titled "How, When, and Why Bad Apples Spoil the Barrel: Negative Group Members and Dysfunctional Groups".

According to a 2015 Harvard Business School study titled "Toxic Workers", swiftly removing a toxic hire can save an organization up to $12,500. Beyond the financial cost, the study highlights the broader impact on productivity at work: 80% of employees reported losing time worrying about a colleague's behavior, 78% felt their commitment to the organization declined, and 63% lost time trying to avoid the stressor. These figures suggest how toxic behaviors can cripple overall team productivity, creating a disjointed and unhappy workforce.

➤ *The Organizational Impact*

The damage from toxic workplace cultures has a significant impact at the organizational level, manifesting behaviors such as absenteeism, quiet quitting and a marked decline in productivity. It reflects an environment where individuals withdraw emotionally and mentally from their roles as a form of self-preservation against the relentless demands of a workplace that neither appreciates nor rewards their efforts.

Whether it's through increased sick leave, skipping crucial meetings, or creatively avoiding the office, these patterns of avoidance are telltale signs of a deepening disconnect for employees with their roles and the organization. This is highlighted in the Oak Engage's Toxic Workplace Report of 2023, which notes that 43% of employees attribute poor attendance directly to negative workplace cultures.

Companies like Amazon serve as a stark example of this. Internal leaks have shown that Amazon's hourly employees face a staggering turnover rate of 150%. The issue of regretted attrition at Amazon, where employees choose to leave on their own, paints an even grimmer picture. It happens at twice the rate of unregretted attrition, which occurs when employees are let go due to performance or other reasons. This highlights a serious problem: the organization is losing valuable talent. Across different levels within Amazon, this regretted attrition ranges between 69.5% and 81.3%, which points to a systemic issue rather than an isolated problem. When these internal figures became public, Amazon faced a wave of scrutiny, forcing them to take a hard look at their culture and retention strategies. Amazon's example clearly shows how toxic workplace environments can take a heavy toll on any organization over a period of time.

But the financial damage doesn't stop there. Toxic cultures can also severely damage an organization's reputation, something much harder to quantify but just as crucial. Organizations known for having negative work environments find it difficult to attract and retain top talent.

The impact of a poor reputation can extend far beyond the surface. Public scandals, like those involving harassment or bullying, can shatter consumer trust and shake investor confidence. A 2021 report from the Australasian Center for Corporate Responsibility (ACCR) highlights how this is becoming a growing concern among investors. They are increasingly worried about the risks that workplace misconduct poses to businesses and are calling for companies to be more transparent and accountable in addressing these issues. Legal risks also loom large, as toxic workplaces often result in lawsuits related to unsafe conditions or harassment. All of these can damage an organization's financial health, affecting its long-term market standing and impact on customer loyalty. In an increasingly competitive job market, where workplace culture often matters more to candidates than salary, a tarnished reputation can be a heavy price to pay for organizations.

The bottom line is clear: if a business wants to thrive and succeed in the long run, it needs to thrive and succeed with its people. Addressing the workplace culture is not something that can be put on the backburner. It needs everyone's continuous focus and attention.

The Need for Restoration

Companies tackling the tough job of fixing toxic workplace cultures often discover that traditional HR strategies simply fall short. To understand why, think of an organization's culture as an old tree. Over time, if the roots are not nourished and properly cared for, the tree starts to wither. It may still stand tall, but its spirit fades. The leaves fall, and the branches lose their strength. The same thing happens in organizations. The toxicity spreads through the roots, slowly eroding what once made the culture strong and spirited. To revive that tree, one wouldn't just trim the branches or paint the trunk; one would have to dig deep, address the state of the roots, and bring them back to life. That's exactly what Cultural Restoration entails.

Culture Restoration, at its core, serves as the antidote to the deep-rooted toxicity that has infiltrated organizational cultures. It is a structured process that delves deep into the organization, addressing the actions and behaviors that have allowed the toxicity to grow. Through this process, an organization can start to transform, shifting its focus from surviving to truly thriving.

This process begins with a single choice: the courage to change. Just like a tree shedding its damaged branches to make space for new life, when organizations are courageous enough to change and focus on cultural restoration, they begin to shed the toxic habits that have been holding them back over the years. This makes way for a healthy, meaningful, and connected workplace where everyone is positively engaged and works collaboratively to transform results for the organization.

Chapter 1

Restoring Cultures

Before we start looking into culture restoration, let us spend some time looking at various other forms of restoration that we might encounter in our lives, what we can learn from them and how we can connect and apply it to the restoration of workplace cultures.

Restoration in Art

As you walk through the halls of the Rijksmuseum in Amsterdam, you will come face-to-face with Rembrandt's majestic painting, "*The Night Watch.*" In 1715, it was trimmed on all sides and cut down to fit a space in Amsterdam's Town Hall, which meant that parts of the original artwork, including some figures, were lost forever. Later, during World War II, the painting faced an even greater threat. To protect it from the Nazis, the entire piece was rolled up and hidden in an underground cave, causing the canvas to warp and deform. While past restoration attempts have worked to repair these damages, none have been as comprehensive as the current project, aptly named "*Operation Night Watch.*"

This restoration which began in 2019 and even continues today, aimed to bring the painting as close to its original form as possible, using advanced technology and the expertise of conservators. This project isn't only about making the painting look new again. It's about preserving the integrity of the artist's original vision while using modern methods to stabilize the work for future generations. Every decision made by the team of restorers is a delicate balance between restoration and respecting the past. Much like the restoration of "The Night Watch," the restoration of an organization's culture involves a similar process of careful examination. Through this lens, we begin to see how the restoration of art mirrors the complex journey organizations face when restoring their culture.

Transparency is an essential part of the process, whether it's in art or in organizations. The beauty of "Operation Night Watch" is that it's being conducted in full view of the public, inviting people to witness the restoration firsthand. This openness builds trust and invites engagement. In organizations, transparency plays a similar role. When leadership openly communicates about the changes taking place and how they align with the organization's core values, it builds trust. Employees feel included in the transformation rather than having it imposed upon them. They become part of the process, which strengthens the sense of shared ownership and makes the cultural restoration more effective.

But restoration doesn't end with a single effort. Just as "The Night Watch" will continue to require ongoing care to keep it intact for future generations, an organization's culture needs regular attention to stay relevant and strong. This ongoing commitment to both preservation and progress is what keeps organizations, like timeless works of art, thriving for years to come.

Restoration in Nature

Restoration isn't limited to art – it's a concept that runs deep in the natural world around us. Exploring these parallels gives us a richer understanding of the process, its scope, and the potential impact it can have. One striking example is ecological restoration, which offers a powerful metaphor for how broken systems can be fully restored.

Take WWF Malaysia's Forest Restoration project, for instance. This initiative, outlined under the 12th Malaysia Plan (2021–2025), focused on restoring degraded forest areas to bring back their ecological functions and improve the well-being of the communities that depend on them. Key steps included assessing forest loss, understanding the potential for restoration, and engaging local communities to get them on board with conservation efforts.

One standout aspect of this is the Rajang-Belawai-Paloh delta, where they aimed to protect nearly 9,000 hectares of mangrove forests, vital for the survival of the Irrawaddy dolphins and the local fishing industry. In addition, they planned to rehabilitate 20 hectares of mangrove land while empowering local communities with workshops that teach sustainable conservation practices. This community involvement played a critical role in ensuring the long-term success of these efforts.

Through these comprehensive restoration efforts, WWF Malaysia healed the environment bringing both immediate benefits to people and lasting gains for the ecosystem around it. The parallels to organizational culture are clear- just as all elements must be assessed for damage and losses in nature, the same needs to be done for restoring organizational culture as well. We need to assess why people left the organization or why employees are disengaged and unhappy.

People and community are at the core of WWF's restoration work, just as people must be at the heart of cultural restoration in any organization. This isn't something leadership can do alone; it requires collective participation, where everyone in the system takes responsibility and ownership in the process of restoration and in making it sustainable over the long-term.

Restoration in Urban Spaces

Urban restoration provides another meaningful metaphor for culture restoration. It involves taking neglected spaces and transforming them into spirited, relevant centers of activity. Take the example of the High Line in New York City, a project that began in 2006 and continued in phases well into 2019, with additional extensions added even in 2023. It perfectly demonstrates the power of thoughtful restoration. Originally, the High Line was an abandoned railway track running through Manhattan's West Side. Over the years, it had fallen into disrepair, a remnant of an industrial era left to decay. But then came the vision to turn this forgotten structure into something new: something that could serve the community in ways no one had imagined before.

Today, the High Line is a dynamic public park that attracts millions of visitors each year. What was once a rusty old railway track is now a green, elevated space filled with art, culture, and nature, linking neighborhoods and creating a sense of connection in the city.

This idea of transforming a deteriorating structure into something that engages and revitalizes a community is at the core of both urban restoration and culture restoration. Just like the High Line project, restoring an organization's culture starts with recognizing the original strengths and values that made it successful in the first place. The process involves reimagining how those values can be adapted to today's realities and needs. Through this kind of thoughtful restoration, just the High Line, an organization can shift from a place of stagnation to one of growth and success.

What Culture Restoration Entails

With the different snapshots of restoration we've explored, it's time to take a closer look at what it really means to restore an organization's culture. Just like bringing an old building back to life, carefully restoring a painting to its original beauty, or restoring the natural world around us, restoring a culture that has been damaged by toxicity is about going back to its core. It's about reconnecting with the values that once made the organization thrive.

Culture Restoration is more than a quick fix. The distinction between repair and restoration is essential here. While repair may focus on temporary solutions, like improving communication or lifting morale, real restoration digs deeper. It reaches into those toxic pockets that might have quietly taken hold in even the healthiest environments. These pockets often form over time, shadowed by unexamined behaviors and unchecked leadership practices. Left unaddressed, they gradually weaken the organization from within, leading to toxicity. To fully restore an organization's culture, we need to identify and examine the underlying, deeper systemic areas to ensure the cultural roots are healthy and able to support new growth.

This transformation process requires more than just a broad, one-size-fits-all solution. It demands a clear and intentional focus, involving interventions that identify those toxic pockets and tackle them head-on. The goal is to create an organization where every action and behavior, from top leadership to frontline operations, is connected and aligned with the organization's core values and strategy. When this kind of connection and alignment occurs, it strengthens and revitalizes the organization. It creates a foundation where people are genuinely empowered, ideas are exchanged openly, and there is a clear sense of purpose driving the work. Conversations don't feel forced or awkward; they seem natural, filled with positive energy and focus. When culture that has been thoughtfully rebuilt with trust, empathy, and inclusion, the organization flourishes with people and results thriving together.

Trust at the Core

Trust is at the core of any restored organization. It's the invisible thread that holds everything together, the element that gives employees the confidence to speak openly, collaborate freely, and feel safe in their roles. Without trust, the culture of an organization can quickly become toxic. Reflecting on our experiences, when we encountered a workplace lacking trust, the atmosphere was noticeably tense. People started to hold back, afraid to express their ideas or concerns because of fear- fear of judgment, fear of retribution, or fear of making mistakes.

When we delve into the neuroscience of trust, we really start to understand why it's so important for restored organizations. There's a fascinating link between trust and how our brains respond to it. Neuroscientific research tells us that when we experience trust, the brain releases oxytocin, often referred to as the "bonding hormone." Oxytocin creates feelings of connection, cooperation, and empathy, which explains why high-trust environments are more collaborative and innovative. Chemically, our brains work better when trust exists. Conversations flow effortlessly, collaboration feels natural, and problems are solved more quickly.

Neuroscientist Paul J. Zak has shown through his research that employees in high-trust organizations report significantly more energy, engagement, and productivity. In fact, those working in environments rich in trust were found to be 50% more productive than their counterparts in low-trust settings.

Another significant impact of Zak's research lies in how it affects employee loyalty. In high-trust organizations, people are much more likely to stick around, with 50% or more employees planning to stay with their employer for the next year and 88% willing to recommend their organization to family and friends. This kind of loyalty can't be fabricated or forced- it grows naturally from a foundation of trust and mutual respect.

Organizations like Great Place to Work™ (GPTW) have shown us the immense impact of placing trust at the heart of workplace culture. GPTW highlights three key dimensions that form the foundation of a high-trust organization: credibility, respect, and fairness. When employees see leaders as honest and capable, feel valued both personally and professionally, and view policies as equitable, trust becomes a natural outcome. This trust drives collaboration, sparks innovation, and boosts employee satisfaction.

Michael C. Bush, CEO of GPTW, often emphasizes that trust starts at the top. Leaders need to demonstrate transparency, follow through on their commitments, and align their actions with the organization's values. By addressing trust gaps, organizations can create truly inclusive workplaces for all, where every individual feels seen and valued.

The benefits of high-trust cultures extend far beyond improved morale. GPTW's extensive global research, which covers over 100 million employees in 170 countries, shows that organizations with strong trust foundations enjoy measurable advantages. Employees in these environments report 60% being more productive, 74% experiencing less stress, and 106% staying more energized. This level of engagement elevates individual performance and strengthens the entire organization, making it more attractive to top talent and helping them stay ahead of the competition.

Heart of Empathy

At the heart of a restored organization, you find empathy, creating an environment where everyone feels truly valued and understood. When empathy is absent, people often feel isolated and unsupported, motivation plummets, and one doesn't feel safe to speak up. We both have seen firsthand how this breeds behaviors like micromanagement, bullying, and humiliation, damaging one's self-worth.

Restoring empathy is essential to healing this kind of damage. When empathy becomes a guiding principle in an organization, it transforms how people communicate and work together. As empathy starts to take root, the walls created by toxic behaviors begin to crumble, replaced by a supportive, restored environment where people are motivated to contribute. But how do we make this happen?

Empathy is contagious, as Stanford professor Jamil Zaki highlights in his book "The War for Kindness". People naturally conform to the behaviors they see around them, whether positive or negative. When employees witness acts of kindness, cooperation, or understanding, they are more likely to mirror those behaviors themselves.

This is aligned with the phenomenon of mirror neurons. In the context of an organization, mirror neurons play a key role in spreading empathy. When someone witnesses a colleague offering support or engaging in a thoughtful act, their brain mirrors that behavior, encouraging them to feel and even act in a similar way. This natural mirroring is how empathy can spread organically in organizations, influencing others and creating an environment where compassion becomes the norm.

The O.C. Tanner 2024 Global Culture Report shows how empathy creates a powerful ripple effect, helping employees feel seen, valued, and truly fulfilled. Employees who view both their leader and organization as empathetic, report significantly higher satisfaction with their workplaces, feeling more connected and motivated. This highlights how a culture infused with empathy can increase retention and overall contribute to organizational success.

Satya Nadella, the CEO of Microsoft, famously said that *"empathy is a muscle that needs to be stretched,"* and this mindset has driven a major cultural shift at Microsoft. When Nadella took over as CEO in 2014, Microsoft was grappling with a deeply entrenched, siloed culture that prioritized competition over collaboration. Innovation was stagnating, and employee morale was low. Recognizing the need for fundamental change, Nadella introduced a new ethos built around empathy, collaboration, and a "growth mindset" inspired by Carol Dweck's groundbreaking work.

This cultural evolution invigorated Microsoft from within. Employees were no longer stuck in a "know-it-all" mindset but were instead encouraged to become "learn-it-alls". This new approach created a workplace where curiosity thrived, ideas flowed freely, and teams worked together to solve problems creatively. As Nadella articulated in his book Hit Refresh (2017), empathy is the foundation for meaningful innovation. By showing empathy and understanding the needs of others, teams could build products and solutions that address real-world challenges.

These changes led to a significant improvement in employee engagement at Microsoft, with metrics showing a 30% increase between 2014 and 2022. Employees felt more connected to their work and to each other, fueling a surge in creativity and productivity. Microsoft's market capitalization skyrocketed from around $300 billion in 2014 to over $2 trillion by 2021. This extraordinary growth illustrates how empathy, when integrated fully into a business, can be instrumental in driving financial success and market dominance for an organization.

Inclusion as a Catalyst

Inclusion in a restored organization works hand in hand with empathy. While empathy helps us understand each person better, inclusion ensures that every person, regardless of background, feels seen, heard, and valued. It's about creating an environment where diverse voices can contribute meaningfully, and decisions reflect a broad range of perspectives.

In toxic workplaces, inclusion is often sorely lacking. Some employees may feel marginalized or ignored, leading to disengagement and stagnation. We have both been in environments where our ideas were dismissed, our voices unheard, and a sense of belonging felt out of reach. It's a deeply isolating feeling that affects not just individuals but the entire organization. When individuals feel that their contributions are overlooked, perhaps because of biases around race, gender, or age, it stifles creativity and damages morale. This creates a negative cycle- people become less engaged, leading to a decline in innovation, collaboration, and performance. The organization becomes rigid, unable to adapt or grow because it fails to embrace the diversity of thought that inclusion brings.

Inclusion is vital in breaking this toxic cycle and restoring an organization. When an organization embraces inclusion and encourages all voices to be heard, it creates a culture of belonging. Employees feel respected and empowered, knowing their perspectives matter. It is compelling to explore how deeply this resonates on a neurological level. When employees feel included, their brains release chemicals like oxytocin and dopamine- both associated with positive feelings and a sense of safety. This enhances personal well-being and boosts team performance. Inclusion acts as a catalyst for this restoration, accelerating the transformation of a toxic culture into one where collaboration, innovation, and growth can truly thrive.

The impact of inclusion is also measurable and deeply connected to an organization's success. Research shows that companies with inclusive cultures are significantly more likely to achieve strong business outcomes. A 2021 report by Boston Consulting Group highlights that organizations fostering inclusivity are twice as likely to meet or surpass financial goals, and are more innovative and adaptable. This environment of respect and value for every employee's contribution fuels not only performance but also retention and engagement. A 2020 Glassdoor survey revealed that 76% of job seekers prioritize a diverse and inclusive workplace when evaluating job opportunities, emphasizing how crucial inclusion is for attracting top talent.

An insightful example of an inclusion-driven culture is Singtel, a leading telecom headquartered in Singapore. Singtel has made significant strides in creating a truly inclusive environment, where women account for 33% of their workforce and 31% are in management. In addition, the Singtel Board of Directors and Management Committee are also women and industry-leading, at 46% and 30%, respectively. Their diverse workforce spans four generations, with Gen Z at 20%, Gen Y at 45%, and Baby Boomers and Gen X at 35%. Additionally, employees at the Singtel Group come from 100 different nationalities. This multi-generational and multinational mix of their workforce underscores the importance of fostering inclusion at Singtel. Its inclusion in the Bloomberg Gender-Equality Index for the fifth consecutive year in 2023 shows its commitment to diversity and inclusion efforts. In 2023, Singtel was also named the world's sixth strongest telecom brand in Brand Finance's Telecoms 150 list, which ranks the most valuable and strongest telecom brands globally.

This example shows how inclusion can transform a workplace- not just through gender diversity but also through generational diversity- benefiting both the people who work there and the organization's overall success.

Leadership's Role in Cultural Restoration

When an organization strives to restore its culture and create an environment where trust, empathy, and inclusion thrive, the role of leadership is an important one.

Leaders are the ones who set the tone and shape the culture. They create conditions where people feel respected and motivated to contribute. This is why the kind of leadership that focuses on human connection and resilience is key to restoring an organization's culture. It's through genuine care and understanding that leaders can guide their teams through challenges and periods of change and help them feel supported along the way.

A core aspect of this kind of leadership is the ability to connect with others on a personal level. Leaders who listen, empathize, and build trust naturally foster collaboration, making it easier for employees to engage with their work and with one another. The result is a culture that feels more open, inclusive, and dynamic.

Additionally, great leaders know how to stay composed during difficult times, which helps their teams remain focused and confident. By modeling resilience, leaders encourage others to tackle challenges with determination. This calm and resilient style of leadership is what enables an organization to grow in a healthy and sustainable way.

To truly grasp the impact of leadership on an organization's culture, let's consider the contrasting leadership styles of Travis Kalanick, former CEO of Uber, and Piyush Gupta, former CEO of DBS Bank. Both these leaders guided highly successful companies, yet the cultures they fostered were vastly different- and the results speak for themselves.

Under Kalanick's leadership, Uber was known for its rapid expansion and aggressive approach to market dominance. From the outside, it looked like an organization built on innovation and success, but internally, the atmosphere was quite different. Kalanick's emphasis on hyper-competitiveness led to a work environment filled with pressure, where ethical considerations often took a backseat. Employees reported a toxic culture, marked by harassment, fear, and high turnover. This relentless drive for success overshadowed the well-being of the team, creating an environment where trust was scarce, and ultimately, the cracks in Uber's culture became visible to the world. The consequences were significant, leading to public scandals, legal challenges, and the departure of Kalanick himself.

On the other hand, we have Piyush Gupta, whose leadership style upholds empathy, inclusivity, and social responsibility. When Gupta took the helm of DBS in 2009, he set out to transform the institution from a traditional banking organization into one of the most innovative, respected and strongest banks in the world.

Gupta's leadership was deeply anchored in purpose-driven banking. Early in his tenure, he emphasized DBS's unique legacy of contributing to Singapore's industrialization and societal development. This history aligned seamlessly with his vision of stakeholder capitalism that included achieving profitability while serving broader societal needs. Gupta embedded customer-centricity into the bank's culture, creating a renewed sense of purpose that motivated employees and strengthened trust among customers and communities.

To build empathy and inclusion within the organization, Gupta introduced initiatives focused on employee well-being and diversity. DBS established an Employee Experience Council, which addressed key aspects of engagement such as workload management, onboarding new hires, and recognition programs. Furthermore, the bank launched its Women Leadership Program to develop a strong pipeline of senior women leaders. These initiatives reflected Gupta's commitment to creating a workplace that values diverse perspectives and ensures every employee feels supported and motivated.

These examples of leadership at Uber and DBS highlight the stark differences between growth strategies focused on short-term gains versus those that prioritize its people and culture. Leaders like Gupta show that it's possible to achieve tremendous success without sacrificing the well-being of employees or compromising on the organization's values.

Now that we recognize what a restored organization looks like and what it entails, the next question is: How do we start on this journey toward culture restoration?

Chapter 2

The Path to Restoration

For a long time, we searched for an approach that could genuinely help organizations assess their culture and restore it to a place of fulfillment, growth and overall greatness. We saw how restoration could benefit organizations, yet the path to get there was far from clear. It took patience, detailed discussions, and lots of insights to finally get some clarity on this.

This exploration started with conversations with peers, colleagues, and friends across different industries that brought us face-to-face with echoes of our own experiences. Some of these stories came out in long chats over coffee; others were confided in quiet, vulnerable moments with trusted friends; and some came from friends of friends, people we hadn't even met but whose stories felt like they could've been our own. We particularly remember a coffee chat with an individual who had endured an intensely toxic work environment. *"Every time I logged on, I felt like a target was on my back,"* they shared openly. *"No matter how hard I tried, it was never enough. Eventually, I stopped trying. I stopped caring."*

We could see ourselves in these stories, feeling that same exhaustion, that same helplessness. The more we listened, the more we realized that each story we heard and every person we interacted with, reflected a workplace culture scarred by toxicity that drained energy, self-worth, and motivation. Restoring these cultures demanded something deeper- a shift that would positively transform these workplaces to thrive once again.

This is when we began experimenting with the initial concept of Restored Leadership, focusing on leaders as a catalyst to transform these cultures. Our aim was to encourage leaders to take a step back, reflect on their own journeys, and address issues that may have drained their passion, eroded their trust, or left them feeling disconnected. By 2022, we began a detailed exploration of The Restored Leadership with a clear purpose: to guide leaders through genuine self-reflection and equip them with the tools needed to create supportive, positive workspaces, beginning at the very top.

But as our research deepened, so did our perspective. When we started to sketch out the traits of a restored leader, we realized the scope of our work had to expand. We discovered that while the restoration of leadership was essential, it was merely a starting point. A restored leader could certainly spark change, but for that change to be meaningful and lasting, the entire organization needed restoration, reaching every team, every department, and every individual.

This realization shifted everything for us. Building on the foundation of Restored Leadership, we began envisioning what a "Restored Organization" could truly be- a workplace thriving together with its people and results. Our focus turned to creating a practical framework to help organizations find ways to humanize workplace cultures and transform results.

We reflected on the attributes often absent in the workplaces we had encountered- respect, trust, ownership, and a genuine sense of listening to understand others. While these attributes were frequently included in mission statements and prominently displayed, they lacked meaningful application in practice. We wanted to change this. And so, inspired by our experiences, the powerful stories shared by others, and the insights we gained, the framework started to take shape.

Beyond FLOW

Moving forward with our efforts, we initially turned to the FLOW framework. It seemed like a solid place to start. Standing for Feedback, Listening, Ownership, and Winning, FLOW aimed to provide a foundation for organizations to begin their journey towards restoration.

In the early days, we conducted several sessions with different teams based on the principles of FLOW. However, as the process unfolded, it became clear that FLOW, while valuable in certain aspects, wasn't enough to address the deeper cultural issues that often plague organizations.

A key challenge was that the framework's emphasis on personal ownership and winning unintentionally reinforced competition rather than collaboration. In an already tense environment, this approach sometimes led to increased divisions, as individuals focused on their personal gains rather than working towards a collective solution. What was intended to empower employees often fell short of building the collaborations needed to sustain long-term results.

Another challenge with FLOW was its heavy focus on leadership development, often prioritizing personal growth and performance. While it's true that better leaders can inspire positive change, the framework didn't fully account for the structural and systemic factors that could contribute to a toxic culture. A leader might become more skilled at giving and receiving feedback, or taking ownership of their work, but without addressing the deep-rooted norms and behaviors that shape the entire organization, these changes don't last long. It's like treating the symptoms of an illness, without understanding the root causes of it.

Moreover, the framework's individual-centric approach tended to exclude the wider organization from the change process. Cultural transformation can't be the responsibility of just a few leaders. It needs to be a shared endeavor, involving people at all levels, from frontline employees to senior executives. Without this inclusive approach, efforts to drive change become fragmented. Some teams may embrace new behaviors, while others remain stuck in old patterns, creating a fragmented culture across the organization. This can lead to improvements that can feel piecemeal and temporary, rather than it being a full restoration of an organization's culture.

The FLOWER Framework™

Over the next two years, we worked on developing a more all-encompassing framework- one that would tackle the many facets of organizational culture and lead to sustainable restoration. In addition to insights that we gained from others' stories and our own experiences, we got deeper understanding from research, neuroscience and from examples of forward-thinking organizations and leaders.

Through conversations and in-depth interactions with over 100 leaders globally, we began to understand the complexities of organizational culture and noticing patterns that were similar. Leaders shared openly about the challenges they faced with employee engagement and productivity and often highlighted how distinct subcultures within their organizations collectively shaped and drove their broader culture. These insights, combined with our previous reflections on FLOW, laid the foundation for what would become the FLOWER framework™.

For an organization to truly "restore" its culture, it needs to look closely at the subcultures within it, much like examining the petals of a flower. A flower is only seen as lively and healthy when each petal is equally bright and full of life. If even one petal is damaged or lacking in color, the entire flower is seen as withering. The same is true for organizations as well. The framework gives a structured approach aimed at restoring the core subcultures so that, just like the petals in a flower, the organization can bloom to its full potential.

We started with a focus on self and teams, leading to the creation of the first four petals: Fulfilling, Listening, Ownership, and Well-being. These address the essential challenges and needs of individuals and teams towards full restoration, providing a clear foundation for fulfillment and collaboration across the organization.

As we broadened our exploration to consider the whole organization, the other two petals emerged: Enterprising and Results-Based, bringing in critical elements essential for broader organizational success and growth.

Together, these six petals form the framework, offering a holistic path to restoration. What makes this approach unique is its adaptive nature. It isn't a rigid or a step-by-step process. Instead, it's non-linear, recognizing that organizations don't all follow the same path to restoration. Each petal can be addressed in any order depending on where the most urgent needs lie. This flexibility allows organizations to start where they feel the most pain and adapt the framework based on their unique needs. The interconnectedness of the petals ensures that changes in one area will naturally ripple across through the others, creating a dynamic, ongoing process of restoration that touches every aspect of the organization.

Fulfilling Culture

As we started to unravel the framework, we begin with the first petal "fulfilling culture". This aspect is critical to any organization's success and lies at the heart of building a thriving and restored workplace. A fulfilling culture is what makes employees feel that their work has meaning, that they are valued, and that they are contributing to something larger than themselves. Without it, employees often find themselves trapped in a cycle of disengagement, feeling disconnected from the organization's mission and purpose. The absence of this fulfillment creates an environment where morale slips, turnover rises, and productivity takes a hit.

Research has consistently shown that when employees feel a sense of fulfillment in their roles, they are more engaged and the benefits ripple across the organization. Companies with high employee engagement often see a notable rise in productivity and even profitability. Gallup's 2023 research on employee engagement reveals some striking insights. Companies with highly engaged teams see a 23% increase in profitability and an 18% rise in productivity compared to those with less engaged employees. These numbers clearly show how a fulfilling culture can drive success throughout an organization.

Neuroscience also offers fascinating insights into why a fulfilling culture matters so much. When employees find meaning and satisfaction in their work, their brains release dopamine, the neurotransmitter responsible for feelings of pleasure and reward. This natural boost in dopamine enhances motivation, sharpens focus, and increases cognitive function. Essentially, when people feel fulfilled, they tend to be more focused and be better equipped to solve problems. This neural response is part of what makes a fulfilling culture so powerful as it helps individuals perform at their best while feeling more engaged and motivated in what they do.

Listening Culture

The second petal of the framework is "listening culture". This involves creating a space where every voice is heard and valued, and feedback is truly integrated into how the organization operates. When a listening culture is missing, it's easy for employees to feel alienated. They may feel that their input doesn't matter, and that frustration can quickly spread throughout the workplace. This creates an environment where enthusiasm fades, engagement falters, and dissatisfaction becomes the norm. A toxic culture can take root when people feel this sense of being unheard and unvalued.

On the other hand, when a listening culture is present, it creates a sense of respect and belonging. When organizations make listening to understand a part of their culture, it leads to profound shifts in how employees feel about their roles and the workplace itself.

From a psychological standpoint, a listening culture also reduces stress and creates an open environment. Employees who know they can speak up without fear of retribution are more likely to voice concerns early, preventing small issues from growing into larger, systemic problems. When people know their voices are respected, they are far more likely to engage in meaningful conversations that drive positive change.

In a listening culture, this sense of attention and understanding leads to what scientist's call *"physiological synchrony,"* where team members' brain activity starts to align with others during positive interactions with them. This synchrony builds deeper cooperation and enhances team cohesion, creating an environment where people are more likely to work together harmoniously and productively. When employees know they are genuinely being listened to, trust grows, and that trust becomes the foundation for a healthier and more engaged workplace.

Ownership Culture

Delving deeper into the framework, the next petal is "ownership culture". An ownership culture encourages people to take initiative, contribute meaningfully, and invest fully in the organization's success. When employees feel ownership in their work, they engage with a deeper sense of purpose.

A lack of this, on the other hand, can leave employees feeling detached and disengaged. Work might feel burdened, accountability drops, and a toxic environment can begin to take hold. In this kind of environment, people may be more inclined to pass blame or sidestep responsibility.

A study published in the Journal of Applied Psychology (2015) found that when employees experience psychological ownership, they are 30–50% more likely to engage in innovative behavior and take more initiative. When employees feel a sense of ownership over something, whether it's a project or their role within the company, they begin to see it as part of their identity. This connection activates neural pathways tied to their identity, making them more invested in the outcome. It's no longer just a task they're completing; it's something they care about on a personal level. This sense of "this is mine" makes employees feel more motivated and connected by a genuine commitment towards their own success and the success of the organization.

Well-being Culture

Next, we explore the petal of a "well-being culture". A culture of well-being goes far beyond offering quick fixes like fitness resources or health incentives. While these programs are helpful, true well-being is about creating an organizational culture where people can show up as their full selves, feeling accepted and fully supported in their holistic well-being. Maslow's Hierarchy of Needs shows us that for anyone to reach their full potential, basic needs like security and belonging must be fulfilled. In the workplace, this means creating an environment where employees don't feel drained or overwhelmed but instead feel energized and supported.

Chronic stress shrinks areas of the brain like the hippocampus, which is responsible for memory and learning. This makes it harder for people to retain information, adapt to new challenges, or come up with creative solutions. A well-being culture can help protect against these negative effects by promoting practices among employees such as purposeful work, giving flexibility in working hours and granting access to holistic wellness resources. These practices keep employees engaged and productive, ensuring they are performing at their best without burning out.

The financial benefits of creating a well-being culture are also hard to ignore. According to the World Health Organization (WHO) in 2019, for "every dollar" invested in well-being programs, companies can expect a return of "4 to 6 dollars". This ROI comes from improved productivity, fewer sick days, and reduced turnover. Additionally, the Return on Well-being Report by Wellhub found that in 2024, 95% of companies reported positive returns from their wellness programs, an increase from 90% in 2023.

Enterprising Culture

With the next petal in the framework "enterprising culture", the focus is on innovation, risk-taking, and adaptability. Organizations that have an enterprising culture tend to be more adaptable and resilient as they encourage employees to explore new ideas while allowing them to take smart risks. When employees know they have the freedom to try new approaches, it sparks creativity and helps them feel more connected to their work. When there are no opportunities for innovation, employees may feel stuck, and over time, this can lead to lower productivity and morale.

A culture that promotes an enterprise mindset, continuous learning, and calculated risk-taking is consistently linked to better productivity, innovation and long-term business success. Gallup's State of the American Workplace report in 2017 shows that employees in innovative and empowering environments are 21% more productive and 59% less likely to seek new jobs.

Neuroscience also provides some helpful insights into this. One key factor is cognitive flexibility, which is the brain's ability to adapt to new information and think creatively. This flexibility is crucial in today's fast-changing business world, where employees need to adapt quickly. The prefrontal cortex (PFC), the part of the brain that is responsible for problem-solving and decision-making, plays a big role here. When organizations create environments that encourage risk-taking and creativity, the PFC gets activated, helping employees adapt to change faster, empowering and motivating them to solve problems innovatively.

Results-Based Culture

We now turn to the final petal of the framework "results-based culture". This is all about creating clarity and accountability around specific, measurable outcomes. In organizations that embrace a results-based culture, employees know what is expected of them, and their efforts are aligned with the organization's bigger goals. It ensures that everyone is working toward those goals, which ultimately enhances their performance and the overall success of the organization.

When there is a lack of clarity about what desired results look like, employees may feel uncertain about their roles and what they're working towards, leading to disengagement. Without this clarity, it becomes harder for employees to see how their contributions tie into the organization's success. This can create a culture of blame, where individuals blame others for lack of results and can lead to a toxic environment.

However, a results-based culture can create the opposite effect. When employees are given clear goals and expectations and they see the connection of their work to the overall success of the organization, they feel encouraged to invest more in their work knowing that their efforts have purpose and meaning. This kind of culture with clear accountability for results, motivates and empowers employees, and enables the organization to move forward with positive intention.

To truly understand the impact of the framework, let's explore its impact on different levels in an organization.

➤ *Individual Level*

At the individual level, the framework profoundly influences how employees experience their work. When people see their contributions being valued, they feel more fulfilled, engaged, and motivated. Clear goals and accountability play a crucial role in this process, tying everything together. When employees understand how their work contributes to the organization's mission, it reduces uncertainty and stress. This clarity allows them to focus on what truly matters, improving both their experience and performance. As a result, individuals perform at their best, innovation increases, and the organization thrives.

➤ *Team Level*

When applied at the team level, the framework encourages open dialogue and active listening within teams, which builds better trust, forming the foundation for long-term organizational success. The concept of collective ownership further strengthens team dynamics. While individual empowerment is important, shared accountability for outcomes means teams are more engaged in collaborative problem-solving and support each other during challenges. This shared responsibility encourages a culture where people and results can thrive together.

➤ *Organization Level*

When implemented across an organization, the framework unifies all cultural elements, creating an environment that humanizes workplaces and transforms results. The framework also ensures comprehensive integration of all aspects of the organization such as employee engagement, productivity, decision-making, innovation and performance. A key aspect of the framework is how it helps in alignment of employee goals and organizational goals. This alignment ensures effective collaboration and connectivity for employees throughout the organization, strengthening the organization's ability to attract and retain top talent, and motivating them to work together in transforming results.

***

The petals of the FLOWER framework™ are designed to be dynamic, encouraging organizations to see cultural restoration as an ongoing journey rather than a quick fix. By understanding all the petals and their interconnectedness within the framework, it allows organizations to create a roadmap that can help them drive sustainable, long-term change towards full restoration.

Next, let's take a closer look at each of the petals in detail and understand their impact on the organization's success.

Chapter 3

Petal One: Fulfilling Culture

What does fulfillment mean to us? This question invites us to reflect on what truly brings a sense of satisfaction and wholeness to our lives. Fulfillment is that deeper feeling of contentment that comes when we are aligned with our values and aspirations. It's about knowing that what we do has meaning and that our efforts are contributing to something worthwhile. This kind of fulfillment is essential for our mental health and well-being. It allows us to see the impact we're making in the world and to take pride in those contributions.

Naturally, this need for fulfillment extends into the workplace. After all, we spend a significant portion of our lives at work, and if we don't feel connected to our roles, it's easy for dissatisfaction to creep in.

As we explored what drives fulfillment at work, we spent countless hours examining reports, sifting through data from our various conversations with leaders, and analyzing studies on organizational culture. As we studied these data points from every angle, they started to reveal new perspectives and insights for us.

One day, in the middle of one of these discussions, we focused on the 2025 Global Culture Report by the O.C. Tanner Institute, and it revealed to us that many organizations still struggle to meet this need. The report introduces the concept of *"Talent Magnets"* for attracting and retaining employees, with a sense of purpose identified as the most significant driver. According to the report, 73% of employees feel a strong sense of purpose when they understand how their work contributes to the organization's broader mission.

This left us pondering a crucial question: *"Why do so many employees still feel unfulfilled in their jobs?"* To explore this further, we spoke with a business leader from a firm in Malaysia who said, *"You'd think it's about the paycheck, but it's more than that. People want to feel they're making a difference, and if that's missing, motivation fades."* He further added, *"If I had more meaning and purpose in my work, I would stay longer in the organization."*

This theme of purpose kept coming up in our conversations with leaders across industries- MNCs, nonprofits, and SMEs alike. Over time, we noticed a common thread: a lack of fulfillment often stems from toxic workplace cultures where employees feel disconnected, undervalued, and stuck in their growth. A fulfilling culture tackles these problems head-on by creating an environment where people feel genuinely connected to the organization's mission and purpose.

Fulfilling Culture within the FLOWER framework™

A fulfilling culture is a vital part of the framework, helping to address toxic issues and restoring the organization's health. It creates an environment where employees feel connected to their work and the organization's mission. This sense of fulfillment leads to greater engagement and encourages open communication, which is the cornerstone of a listening culture.

A fulfilling culture also strengthens an ownership culture within the organization. When employees have a shared purpose, they communicate and collaborate more openly and feel strong ownership to improve the organization. Prioritizing fulfillment also enhances a well-being culture in an organization, ensuring that employees feel productive, are engaged positively, and their health is balanced physically, emotionally, and mentally. In addition, fulfillment drives innovation and creativity, essential for an enterprising culture. In a purposeful environment, employees feel safe exploring new possibilities and ideas, and knowing that their contributions are valued, it helps keep the organization competitive and ahead in the market. Finally, in a results-based culture, fulfillment motivates employees to perform at their best and helps them stay focused and committed toward results.

So, how do we build a fulfilling culture in an organization? Through insights gained from our interviews with various leaders and a deep dive into research, we've identified three key elements essential for building a fulfilling culture:

➢ **Purpose**
➢ **Recognition**
➢ **Career Development**

Let's delve into each of these elements in depth.

Element 1: Purpose

Let's begin with purpose, often regarded as the heartbeat of a fulfilling workplace. Purpose-driven work is what truly fuels a fulfilling culture, bringing employees closer to the "why" behind their roles and creating a powerful connection between their personal values and the organization's mission.

When employees feel connected to a purpose larger than themselves, it taps into something much deeper than external rewards or recognition. It brings a sense of belonging and meaning to their everyday tasks. People are no longer just clocking in and out; they are contributing to something that resonates with them on a personal level. This feeling of alignment can transform the way people approach their work, fueling creativity, passion, and a commitment to excellence.

A study by McKinsey during the Covid-19 pandemic found that two-thirds of employees began to rethink their life's purpose and reassess their careers during that time. This still holds true even today, and many employees are on the lookout for jobs that provide a deeper sense of meaning and purpose. This highlights the importance for organizations to acknowledge and prioritize purpose in their culture if they want to genuinely engage, motivate, and retain their talent.

Neuroscience provides even deeper insights into the importance of purpose in the workplace, further cementing its crucial role in building a fulfilling culture. Research by Robbins & Everitt (2007) and Esposito et al. (2011) shows that engaging in meaningful tasks increases dopamine levels in the brain. This release activates neural pathways that enhance cognitive flexibility, increase motivation, and improve problem-solving skills.

Purposeful work also has a unique impact on the brain's Default Mode Network (DMN), which is involved in self-reflection and future planning. When individuals are connected to a strong sense of purpose, their brain's DMN becomes more active, enhancing their ability to think about the future, make better decisions, and approach problems with more empathy. This increased connectivity helps individuals integrate their thoughts and actions more effectively, allowing them to align their day-to-day work with long-term organizational goals. The result is a more thoughtful, forward-thinking approach to problem-solving and decision-making, benefiting both the individual and the organization.

To understand this better, let's take a closer look at **three key strategies** for effectively restoring purpose in an organization's culture.

1. Role Modeling

A key strategy for restoring purpose in a fulfilling culture is for leaders to role model it for the employees. Purpose activation starts from the top with leaders practicing the right behaviors and creating an environment where employees feel motivated to do the same. When leaders make a conscious effort to do this every day, the workforce becomes more engaged and connected with a common sense of purpose.

One remarkable example of this approach comes from the late Major (Retired) Surajan's leadership at SITA Pest Control in Singapore during the 1990s. Sebastian worked under Major Surajan during that time when pest control was often seen as routine or menial work, lacking deeper meaning. However, Major Surajan believed that the work they did played a critical role in Singapore. *"What you do here matters for the safety and well-being of our society,"* he would tell them, reshaping how they viewed their work.

As Managing Director, he organized regular gatherings where employees could openly share challenges, celebrate successes, and explore how their roles contributed to a larger mission. Giving this space for reflection, he helped all employees realize that their work had a sense of purpose and what they did was impactful.

Every morning Major Surajan would personally meet with Pest Control Officers (PCOs), greet them by their names and show interest in their lives outside work. When he attended the Singapore Pest Management Association (SPMA) meetings as President, he would openly share his perspectives on the organizational challenges and discuss ways to make the organization better. Often, he would ask for feedback from Sebastian and others and show interest in their own aspirations or goals. *"It felt to me that he genuinely cared about me, and I shared with him openly my reflections about work and life,"* Sebastian recalls. This openness showed how Major Surajan cared not just about SITA Pest Control but also about its people and the importance of purpose in life.

When SITA Pest Control ceased operations in Singapore, nearly all employees chose to follow him to his new company, Major's Pest Management Services, which he established in 2003. His ability to role model purpose every day left a lasting impact for everyone, and today his daughter continues his strong legacy forward with the organization.

2. *Authentic Storytelling*

Another effective method to restore purpose within an organization's culture is through authentic storytelling. Authentic stories uniquely connect people to a shared mission in meaningful ways. Leaders can utilize storytelling to reinforce the organization's values, demonstrating how these values manifest in daily work and how they directly impact the broader organization's goals. By sharing real examples of how individual efforts contribute to the organization's success, employees can see the purpose behind their tasks, building motivation and a stronger sense of belonging.

Atlassian, the Australian software organization founded in 2002, has made storytelling an integral part of its culture. One example of this commitment is the "Humans of Atlassian" project, launched during a quarterly hackathon. This initiative captures personal testimonials from employees, sharing moments of kindness, collaboration, and connection within the company. Stories have included everything from colleagues supporting one another during emergencies to simple but meaningful gestures, like replacing a lost tea infuser.

Atlassian also encourages authenticity in its storytelling approach by integrating some of its values such as "Open Company, No Bullshit," "Build with Heart and Balance," and "Be the Change You Seek" into its daily operations, hiring practices, and employee interactions.

Atlassian's storytelling extends beyond internal culture through initiatives like the Engage 4 Good program, formally launched in 2021. This skills-based volunteering program connects employees with non-profit projects aligned with their interest and expertise. Nearly 90% of participants reported feeling a stronger connection to Atlassian's mission after participating. By sharing stories of impact from these projects within the organization and society, Atlassian demonstrates how its work goes beyond business, restoring a deeper sense of purpose and fulfillment in its employees.

3. *Purpose-Driven Initiatives*

Investing in purpose-driven initiatives can help ensure all employees and leaders are fully aligned with the organization's mission. This strategy begins with actively involving employees discovering their own purpose and helping them align it to the organization's mission or purpose. At the same time, leadership plays a critical role in helping embed purpose into the organization's daily practices, and this can help effectively drive both individual motivation of employees and the collective success of the organization.

Unilever, a global leader in consumer goods, exemplifies this commitment to purpose-driven initiatives. Unilever's goal is to embed its purpose "to make sustainable living commonplace" into every layer of the organization. The "Discover Your Purpose" workshop launched in 2018 is one of the ways they've done this by encouraging employees to explore and connect their own personal purpose with Unilever's purpose. By 2023, over 57,000 employees had participated in these reflective workshops, designed to help employees explore their strengths, values, and aspirations while aligning them with Unilever's purpose. A study conducted in partnership with the London School of Economics found that participants reported a 49% increase in intrinsic motivation after these workshops and 25% felt more inspired and connected to their roles, underscoring the workshops' effectiveness.

Leadership at Unilever also plays a vital role in driving its purpose throughout the organization. Initiatives such as "Leading the Unilever Way" (LTUW) focus on equipping senior leaders to model purpose-driven behaviors. By 2023, more than 400 leaders had completed over 18,000 hours of training, embedding and reinforcing Unilever's purpose and values in their teams and daily operations. Both these initiatives show how purpose remains a guiding force in enhancing fulfillment for Unilever's employees and keeping them motivated to drive collective success for the organization.

Element 2: Recognition

Recognition is an equally important aspect of a fulfilling workplace culture. Recognition goes to the heart of how we, as humans, feel valued and appreciated. It touches on a deep psychological need that fuels our motivation and engagement at work. In fact, when we revisited Abraham Maslow's Hierarchy of Needs, it reinforced what we already knew: once our basic needs for safety and belonging are met, we strive for social needs such as the need for respect, recognition, and appreciation.

When employees receive genuine recognition for their efforts, it boosts their self-esteem, supports their growth, and helps assure them that they are making meaningful contributions. This simple act of acknowledgment enhances their motivation toward their work and strengthens their connection to the workplace.

Neuroscience also provides some important insights into this. Recognition satisfies a deep-rooted psychological need for validation and appreciation, which is crucial for motivation and engagement. This need is tied to how our brains are wired, specifically the brain's reward system. When we get recognition, our brains release neurotransmitters like dopamine and serotonin, both of which play key roles in enhancing our mood and overall well-being. This release creates a sense of pleasure and satisfaction, reinforcing the positive behavior that led to the recognition.

This understanding of recognition's psychological impact paves the way for appreciating its broader effects on employee morale. According to the 2024 Gallup and Workhuman study, which tracked the career paths of over 3,400 employees from 2022 to 2024, employees who received high-quality recognition in 2022 were 45% less likely to leave their jobs by 2024. This suggests that, when it comes to recognition, the dopamine-rich recognized behavior can boost individual morale and can significantly influence organizational loyalty.

To understand this better, let's take a closer look at **3 key strategies** for effectively restoring recognition in an organization's culture.

1. *Tie Recognition to Values*

An effective way to make recognition meaningful is to link it directly to the organization's core values. When recognition highlights this, it reinforces the behaviors and actions that contribute to the organization's success. This alignment helps employees see how their work supports the larger mission, making recognition feel purposeful rather than routine.

In this regard, the 2024-2025 Annual Rewards and Recognition (R&R) Report, collaboratively published by SHRM India, Vantage Circle, and Aon, analyzed insights from over 250 companies across 10 industries. The report revealed that 3 out of 4 companies surveyed were looking to leverage Rewards & Recognition (R&R) programs to drive behavioral change and engagement within their organizations. The report also discovered that when organizations were able to better align their R&R programs to their values, mission or purpose, employees were more motivated, and it yielded better results for the organization.

An example of linking recognition to organizational values is Wipro, a leading global technology services and consulting company headquartered in India. Wipro revamped its Recognition and Rewards (R&R) program in 2021 to align it with its five core values: Respect, Responsiveness, Communication, Stewardship, and Trust.

To achieve this, Wipro adopted the AIRE (Appreciation, Incentivization, Reinforcement, and Empowerment) approach. This integrated real-time appreciation of contributions, incentivization through monetary and non-monetary rewards, continuous reinforcement of desired behaviors, and empowerment for recognizing others. The program also featured diverse recognition types in alignment with the values of the organization, such as SPOT Awards for outstanding achievements, Unit Awards for team accomplishments, and Long Service Awards to celebrate employee loyalty.

The results of this initiative have been transformative. From 2021 to 2023, Wipro saw a 97.5% increase in non-monetary awards, such as badges and appreciation tokens, reflecting a positive shift toward its value-based recognition culture. On average, 768 awards were given daily in 2023, amounting to over 553,490 awards in two years- translating to an employee being recognized every 1.2 minutes. The initiative's success was further validated by prestigious accolades, such as the Brandon Hall Group Gold Award for "Best Advance in Employee Recognition Program" in October 2023.

2. Peer Recognition

Another highly effective strategy is implementing a peer recognition system. Instead of relying solely on top-down recognition from managers, peer recognition empowers everyone in the organization to be involved in the process of celebrating the success of their peers. It creates a more inclusive and encouraging environment where all employees, regardless of position, feel seen, heard and appreciated.

For example, Southwest Airlines, headquartered in Texas, demonstrates the successful implementation of peer recognition through its innovative SWAG (Southwest Airlines Gratitude) program, launched in 2018. As one of the largest low-cost carriers in the United States, Southwest Airlines operates with over 76,000 employees (referred to as "Cohearts") across more than 120 destinations. The airline has long prioritized its people-first culture and has integrated peer recognition into its various touchpoints of the employee journey.

The SWAG program empowers employees to recognize and thank each other both formally and informally. Employees can send recognition through a mobile app or physical cards, often accompanied by points redeemable for merchandise, gift cards, or other experiences. Additionally, new hires are introduced to this culture from day one through onboarding experiences that include red-carpet welcomes and personalized gifts.

The results of Southwest's peer recognition strategy are remarkable. By Q3 2023, the SWAG platform had achieved 97% engagement among employees, and the organization had facilitated over 359,000 recognition moments highlighting the effectiveness of peer recognition for purposeful work at Southwest.

3. Personalization

A great way to restore recognition in the workplace is to make it personal. This approach means understanding what motivates each person and tailoring recognition to suit their preferences- whether it's public acknowledgment in a meeting, a thoughtful thank you note, or a reward that aligns with someone's personal interests. When recognition is personalized, it shows employees that they're seen as individuals, which boosts both engagement and motivation.

Disney, headquartered in California, has long been recognized for its employee recognition programs that emphasize personalization. The Walt Disney Legacy Award is indeed one of Disney's most prestigious internal recognition programs. It was launched in 2011 and is awarded to Cast Members who consistently go above and beyond in their work. The winners receive a distinctive blue name tag engraved with "Dream, Create, Inspire," symbolizing their exceptional achievements.

The program is highly personalized as it celebrates individual contributions through tailored rewards. For example, recipients are often surprised by individual ceremonies where they are honored in front of their teams. Additionally, winners are invited to exclusive events or given opportunities that align with their interests and roles within the company. This ensures that recognition feels meaningful and deeply personal. In FY2023, the award event was held for the 23rd time, with ceremonies celebrating exceptional cast members.

The RecognizeNow! Platform, launched globally in 2020, is another internal initiative aimed at cultivating a culture of personalized recognition within Disney. This digital platform allows managers and peers to send personalized notes of appreciation tied to Disney's service standards. The platform enables leaders to align recognition with specific achievements by offering tailored rewards such as additional paid time off or curated experiences. By 2024, employee engagement with the platform remained robust, and Disney continues to use it successfully across the organization.

Element 3: Career Development

Career development plays a vital role in restoring a workplace culture where employees feel truly fulfilled. When an organization invests in its people's development, it sends a clear message that their growth and contributions are valued.

The psychological significance of career development can be understood through self-determination theory, which highlights three core human needs: competence, autonomy, and connection. Introduced by psychologists Edward Deci and Richard Ryan in the 1980s, this theory explains that these needs are fundamental to motivation and well-being. When these needs are met, people are more likely to be motivated, engaged, and satisfied in their work.

Competence refers to the need to feel effective and capable in one's tasks. Employees who have opportunities to develop their skills and grow in their roles are more likely to feel competent. This sense of competence boosts their confidence and motivates them to take on new challenges and excel in their work.

Autonomy, the second element, speaks to the need for employees to feel they have control over their own work. When organizations allow employees to choose their own career pathways, they give employees the freedom to take charge of their professional development.

Connection, the third element, addresses the need for belonging and purpose within the workplace. In a post-COVID world, this sense of connection is significantly important. After years of remote work and isolation, employees now place a higher value on environments where they feel genuinely connected, where they're not just contributors but valued members of a community.

Several studies also highlight the importance of career development. A 2021 survey by Mercer in Southeast Asia found that 43% of employers cited limited career advancement opportunities as a leading cause of employee turnover. This is particularly relevant for mid-career professionals who actively seek career growth and progression. Without clarity on these development paths, talented individuals may continue to leave organizations.

Career development plays a powerful role in building this sense of belonging. When organizations actively support their employees' growth, they are essentially creating a sense of fulfillment in them. As employees grow and advance within the company, they develop a deeper sense of this fulfillment in their roles and the organization itself.

To understand this better, let's take a closer look at **three key strategies** for effectively restoring career development in an organization's culture.

1. *Core Focus*

For any Career Development opportunities to be effective, they must be fully integrated into the organization's core. This means that career growth should be a central part of the organizational ethos, ensuring that every employee understands the significance of continuous learning and personal development. When career development is seen as a core focus, it creates an environment where growth is expected, encouraged, and celebrated.

Hilton, a global leader in hospitality, shows this commitment to career development by making it integrated in the core of the organization. One notable example is the Passport to Success (PTS) program. Launched in 2013, in partnership with the International Youth Foundation, PTS is deeply tied to Hilton's values of Leadership and Teamwork. It began as an instructor-led initiative to bridge skill gaps and has since expanded to include online modules, enhancing its adaptability. Since its inception, PTS has trained over 15,000 young people, both at Hilton properties and within local communities. A survey conducted with 300 supervisors revealed that 80% of PTS participants improved in areas such as teamwork, communication, and confidence. Moreover, the program's effectiveness is reflected in retention rates, with 96% of team members trained under PTS remaining with Hilton for at least six months, and 40% earning promotions.

Hilton further commits to this core focus through initiatives like Lead@ Hilton, which provides tailored programs for employees at every career stage. These initiatives create structured growth pathways, empowering employees to progress from first time managers to seasoned leaders. In 2023 alone, over 300 leaders engaged in these programs were considered for promotion, showing how Hilton's core focus on career development translates into meaningful developmental opportunities for its employees.

2. Mentorship

Ongoing mentorship is yet another vital strategy for enabling career development, providing employees with sustained guidance and support as they navigate their professional growth. By connecting employees with experienced leaders who share knowledge, offer advice, and help them develop their skills, organizations create a strong support system that fosters confidence and commitment. A strong mentorship culture ensures employees feel supported throughout their time at the organization, empowering them to pursue their career goals and setting them up for success.

An organization that has excelled in facilitating ongoing mentorship is Caterpillar Inc., the globally recognized heavy machinery and equipment manufacturer based in the United States. Unlike many companies that offer only short-term mentorship stints, Caterpillar developed a comprehensive program in 2019 where mentorships last between two to three years. This extended timeframe allows for continued and meaningful relationships between mentors and mentees, and helps employees stay fulfilled in their roles. At Caterpillar, mentorship is not only about developing technical skills but also about cultivating leadership qualities, ensuring mentees are well-prepared to advance within the company.

In addition to its long-term mentorship program, Caterpillar has implemented the Engineering Rotational Development Program (ERDP), which has been a key aspect of its talent pipeline since its launch in 2004. Designed to support early-career engineers, the ERDP offers rotational assignments across various engineering disciplines. Mentorship plays a central role in the ERDP, as participants are paired with experienced mentors who guide them through technical challenges and help them in their career planning. Since 2004 and now, Caterpillar has onboarded over 2,000 engineers through this program and in 2023, 189 ERDP participants came from 17 engineering majors and 45 different universities. Through these developmental initiatives, Caterpillar ensures its employees have the resources, guidance, and support needed to be successful in the long term.

3. Internal Mobility

Another key strategy for career development is to promote internal mobility within the organization. When employees have the chance to explore different roles within the organization, they can broaden their skill sets and gain new perspectives. This enhances individual capabilities and benefits the organization by creating a more versatile and adaptable workforce.

Organizations can encourage internal mobility by creating clear pathways for employees to move across departments or take on new challenges that align with their interests and career aspirations. Internal Mobility, coupled with cross-training, allows employees to learn from different functions, making them more equipped to handle diverse tasks and challenges.

To see how this strategy has been effectively applied, let's explore the case of Schneider Electric, a global leader in energy management and automation headquartered in France. In 2019, Schneider Electric launched the Open Talent Market, an AI-driven internal platform that addressed a critical challenge the organization faced: nearly 50% of employees who left the organization cited a lack of internal growth opportunities as a primary reason. The Open Talent Market gave employees visibility of available job postings and short-term projects (often called "gigs") across the company. The platform empowered employees to take control of their career development, providing them with options to move across departments, engage in diverse projects, and build new skills.

Soon after launching the Open Talent Market, the company also partnered with Gloat, a talent marketplace platform that aggregated information from employee profiles and helped to discern their skills and interests. The platform then matched those skills and interests to roles within the organization, creating suggestions for viable career paths as well as guidance to bridge skill gaps to embark on their desired careers.

Within two months of the internal talent marketplace launch, 60% of employees had registered in the system, and more than 2,300 employees were exploring new roles within the company. Through the talent marketplace, the company unlocked nearly 127,000 hours of previously unused talent in just a few weeks. By 2022, over 60,000 employees utilized these platforms.

These findings reveal that platforms like the Open Talent Market and Gloat have successfully created a culture of career mobility within Schneider Electric, allowing employees to transition easily to different roles and be in control of their career development.

***

Over the course of this chapter, we've broken down what it takes to create and sustain a fulfilling culture. By implementing some of the strategies and examples we've shared, you can begin laying a strong foundation for meaningful cultural restoration.

To tie it all together, let's revisit everything through a micro case study that shows how it all comes together in a thriving, restored organization.

Patagonia's Fulfilling Organizational Culture

Founded by Yvon Chouinard in 1973, Patagonia has made a name for itself as an outdoor apparel brand and an organization that deeply values its mission, employee well-being, and sustainable growth.

Purpose

Patagonia's purpose, *"We're in business to save our home planet,"* which was rewritten in 2018, extends beyond traditional business goals, shaping every aspect of its operations toward creating a deeply fulfilling workplace culture. This commitment to environmental responsibility guides decision-making, product design, and employee engagement, ensuring that the purpose is embedded into daily work. Patagonia strengthens this culture by integrating sustainability into its business practices, using recycled materials, encouraging activism, and even offering paid time off for employees to engage in purposeful work.

A standout initiative reinforcing this sense of purpose is the Environmental Internship Program, launched in 1993. This program allows employees to take up to two months off work to volunteer for an environmental organization of their choice while continuing to receive full compensation and benefits.

In 2023, the program demonstrated its lasting impact: 34 employees across 12 stores and one department participated, contributing nearly 10,000 volunteer hours to 43 different environmental organizations. Beyond providing employees with hands-on experience in sustainability, the program deepened their connection to Patagonia's purpose, reinforcing the idea that their work contributes to something bigger and more meaningful.

Recognition

Patagonia's recognition programs are deeply rooted in its values of environmental stewardship and social responsibility. One of Patagonia's key initiatives is its peer-to-peer recognition program, which allows employees to nominate their colleagues for their contributions to environmental efforts, sustainability projects, or community volunteerism. By empowering employees to recognize one another for embodying Patagonia's values, the program nurtures a sense of community and belonging in the workplace.

Patagonia also offers flexible award options as part of its recognition programs. Employees who receive awards can choose from a variety of meaningful rewards, such as gift cards, outdoor adventure experiences, or donations to environmental causes they personally support. This personalized approach ensures that recognition aligns with employees at an individual level while also connecting at the organization level. The impact of these initiatives is evident in Patagonia's employee engagement and satisfaction scores. According to Patagonia's 2023 B Corp Report, 81% to 90% of employees reported high levels of engagement at work, and 91% of employees said they love working at Patagonia.

Career Development

Patagonia places significant emphasis on career development, ensuring ample opportunities for personal and professional growth. Through initiatives like Patagonia University, employees can access workshops, webinars, and other learning resources that align with both organizational goals and individual development. This approach creates a mutual benefit, where employees grow in their roles and the organization retains great talent.

Patagonia's Summit Learning Platform, launched in 2018, has also been a key part of the company's efforts to support internal mobility for its employees. The platform provides access to a wide range of in-person and on-demand professional development opportunities, focusing on areas such as leadership development, purpose-driven work, activism, and product knowledge. By equipping employees with transferable skills, the platform empowers them to prepare for lateral or upward mobility within the company, enabling them to proactively shape their career trajectories.

In addition to formal training, Patagonia's mentorship programs provide guidance and support for employees' career growth. To further support their career advancement, Patagonia also offered tuition reimbursement for approved educational programs, helping employees pursue formal education that enriches their careers further.

Through its commitment to purpose, recognition, and career development, Patagonia has crafted a fulfilling workplace culture that engages employees meaningfully and helps them stay motivated through a common purpose.

In 2022, Yvon Chouinard, in an open letter said, instead of going public, the company was "going purpose". And true to its purpose, they turned the company into a non-profit and gifted 100% of its $3B fortune to it, showing their deep commitment to the planet and environment.

Reflective Assessment

Petal 1: Fulfilling Culture

After reading the chapter, what is your current assessment of your organization's culture?

1. Purpose

What specific strategies do you have in place to help your employees reflect on their own purpose?

....

....

....

In what ways can you enhance this further?

....

....

....

2. Recognition

What methods do you currently use to recognize your employees?

....

....

....

What improvements can be made to make recognition more impactful?

....

....

....

3. Career Growth

How has your organization implemented career mobility and cross-training programs?

....

....

....

In what areas can you further improve these opportunities for your employees?

....

....

....

Chapter 4

Petal Two: Listening Culture

We'd like to start this exploration of a listening culture with a contrast between two distinct workplaces. In one, the energy is unmistakable. People are engaged, conversations flow, and there's a sense of openness in how people interact. Over in one corner, a manager is talking with an employee who's leaning forward, clearly invested in the conversation.

"I think we could save a lot of time if we tried this new process," the employee says. The manager listens closely, nodding and making eye contact, then responds, *"That's a great suggestion. How do you think we can make this work?"*

Now, let's consider the second workplace. Here, the atmosphere feels heavy and tense. People keep to themselves, and conversations, when they happen, are brief and to the point. In a meeting room, an employee nervously raises a concern, saying, *"I've noticed that our current approach is leading to delays."* The manager, without even looking up, replies dismissively, *"Don't waste your time and just do your job,"* and swiftly moves to the next item on the agenda. The employee leaves the meeting looking deflated, knowing from experience that it's pointless to speak up. This is the kind of place where people keep their thoughts to themselves and avoid conflict. They've accepted the fact that no one's really listening, so why bother?

These two workplaces reveal the stark difference between a culture that values listening and a culture of silence. In the first environment, people feel valued and confident that their input matters; in the second, apathy and frustration have set in as feedback goes nowhere.

Listening taps into a basic human need to feel valued and respected. In the workplace, where we spend so much of our time, this need becomes even more important. When people feel genuinely listened to, it validates them. It tells them that their experiences and insights have weight. But when people feel unheard, frustration and disengagement take over. Over time, lack of listening erodes trust, leaving people feeling unimportant and unmotivated. This is especially true in workplaces with toxic cultures.

During the interviews we had, many employees shared their experiences with us, highlighting how lack of listening to understand was a pervasive issue. One individual from Singapore, Sally, shared candidly, *"It felt like no matter what we said, our input was just white noise. I stopped sharing ideas because I knew they'd be brushed aside."* Another, Siew Lin, described the experience as feeling "invisible," and her insights and efforts went entirely unnoticed. These instances reveal how lack of listening does more than just frustrate individuals- it reshapes how employees view their roles within the organization and how it can profoundly affect the organization's culture and effectiveness.

Research from the 2022 study, The Power of Listening at Work by Avraham Kluger and Guy Itzchakov, highlights the profound impact of listening on organizational success. This study reveals that when managers truly listen, it significantly boosts employee job performance and engagement. Employees with attentive managers are more likely to go above and beyond their job duties, contribute meaningfully and have lower intentions to leave their jobs. The study also found that managers who listen actively create an environment where employees feel comfortable speaking up and sharing new ideas.

Additionally, the research emphasizes that listening has a direct, positive impact on organizational commitment. Employees who feel genuinely listened to are not only more satisfied in their jobs but are also more committed to their organizations. These findings show the tremendous value that active listening brings to an organization, affecting everything from individual performance to long-term loyalty and motivation.

Listening Culture within the FLOWER framework™

A listening culture forms the foundation that supports the other petals of the framework. In a fulfilling culture, listening helps organizations truly understand employees' purpose and career aspirations and helps in making recognition more authentic and career growth opportunities more tailored.

Listening powers up an ownership culture by giving employees a voice in decision-making and encouraging them to take more initiative and responsibility. By listening and identifying concerns early, it also supports a well-being culture that proactively addresses mental, emotional, and physical health of all employees. In an enterprising culture, listening creates open spaces for collaboration, allowing diverse perspectives that can fuel innovation. Finally, within a results-based culture, listening also helps organizations better align employee performance goals to results and build better accountability.

So, how do we build a listening culture in an organization? Through insights gained from our interviews with various leaders and a deep dive into research, we've identified three key elements essential for building a listening culture:

> **Active Listening**
> **Open Feedback Channels**
> **Commitment to Inclusion**

Let's delve into each of these elements in depth.

Element 1: Active Listening

Active listening transforms communication from a basic exchange of words into something deeper – a real experience of connection, respect, and trust. The idea was first introduced by Carl Rogers and Richard Farson back in 1957, and it is rooted in humanistic psychology. Rogers, known for his client-centered therapy work, believed that listening wasn't just about hearing someone's words. It meant truly understanding the emotions and perspectives behind them. While this concept started in therapeutic settings, it quickly proved to be just as important in business and leadership.

A 2017 Salesforce study surveyed over 1,500 business professionals on leadership and workplace equality. The findings revealed that employees who felt heard were 4.6 times more likely to do their best work. As we dug deeper to understand this more, we wanted to look at this from a neuroscience perspective. It's one thing to know that being listened to makes people feel motivated, but seeing the actual brain activity behind it adds a new layer of insight.

Neuroscience reveals that when people feel genuinely listened to, specific areas of the brain associated with reward and emotional processing become active. This response, observed through functional magnetic resonance imaging (fMRI), is tied to feelings of pleasure and satisfaction. Beyond nurturing positive emotions, this activation helps reduce stress, creating an optimal environment for cognitive flexibility and creativity. Another aspect involves the prefrontal cortex, responsible for executive functions such as decision making and emotion regulation. When we engage in active listening, this part of our brain works differently. Normally, our brains are wired to predict what someone is going to say next or plan our own response while they're talking. It's an approach where we filter new information based on past experiences or what we expect to hear. But active listening flips that approach. It forces the prefrontal cortex to quiet those impulses so we can focus fully on what the speaker is saying without jumping to conclusions or interrupting. This bottom-up way of processing makes us more open-minded and receptive.

In the workplace, this shift in how we process information can create opportunities for new ideas and collaborative problem-solving. It's one of those things that sound simple but can fundamentally change how teams interact and how solutions are conceptualized.

To understand this better, let's take a closer look at **three key strategies** for effectively restoring active listening in an organization's culture.

1. Reflective Conversations

Embedding active listening in an organization's culture is not always straightforward. One significant challenge is the mental narratives we constantly construct in our minds, where we interpret others' words based on our assumptions, biases, or past experiences. These internal stories can trigger emotions and judgments that cloud our ability to truly listen. Overcoming this requires a shift in mindset- one that encourages us to reframe these narratives and give others our full attention. By reminding ourselves that we might not have the full picture or could be "missing something," we open ourselves up to listen with greater openness and less bias.

To tackle these challenges, structured opportunities for reflective conversations can play a vital role. Reflective conversations encourage people to pause, consider what's been shared, and respond thoughtfully rather than reactively. This approach fosters a deeper level of listening that goes beyond immediate responses, building genuine understanding and empathy. Setting aside time for these types of conversations can make a significant difference across teams, enhancing both communication and collaboration.

In the context of this approach, we'd like to talk about a leader who embodies this approach at every level: Dr. Peggy Crowe, with whom one of us, Nitin, had the privilege of working at Western Kentucky University (WKU) from 2000 to 2002. Peggy was the Assistant Director in the Department of Housing and Residence Life and had a way of listening that set her apart. She embodied the phrase "listen to understand," a quality that was felt by everyone who had the chance to work with her. She led with the belief that reflective conversations required genuine engagement and intentionality. Peggy facilitated spaces where team members and students could reflect on their experiences, articulate their concerns, and feel fully heard.

During the aftermath of 9/11, Peggy's approach became particularly impactful. At a time when many minorities on campus felt unsafe or marginalized, she initiated listening sessions where students could openly share their fears and experiences. These structured conversations went beyond surface-level discussions, providing a safe and supportive environment for individuals to express their concerns. Peggy's ability to listen without judgment and encourage thoughtful dialogue helped ensure trust and understanding, leading to initiatives like "Racism at WKU." This program created a platform for candid conversations about inclusion, allowing participants to reflect on their biases and build bridges across differences to better understand everyone's perspectives.

Peggy also applied this strategy to day-to-day operations. For example, in the "MASTER Plan" initiative- a program designed to help students transition to university life- she made sure every team member had the opportunity to share their ideas and feedback during planning sessions. By integrating reflection and listening into this process, Peggy ensured that everyone felt their voice mattered. This approach enhanced the program's success and strengthened team morale and collaboration.

A lot of organizations have adopted such reflective conversations and successfully incorporated them into their After-Action Reviews (AARs). Even NASA conducts reflective sessions throughout a project's lifecycle rather than just at the end. They brand this approach as "Pause and Learn."

2. *Peer-to-Peer Listening*

Encouraging employees to practice active listening with their peers can significantly improve communication, collaboration, and trust within teams. Peer-to-peer listening can be strengthened through structured activities like team-building exercises, collaborative projects, or even informal check-ins. Research from Gallup (2023) reveals that when employees feel connected with their peers, engagement jumps by nearly 50%, and the overall sense of belonging within the organization strengthens. By integrating active listening into these everyday peer interactions, companies create a culture where everyone feels heard, not just in formal meetings but in the flow of daily conversations.

Here, we explore the example of Reuters, the global news and media organization headquartered in London, UK, which has actively integrated peer listening into its workplace culture. In 2015, Reuters established its Peer Support Network as part of its broader Global Trauma Program, aimed at supporting employees facing work-related stress, trauma, or online harassment. The Peer Network consisted of 48 Reuters staff journalists stationed worldwide, including regions such as Asia, Africa, Middle East, Europe, and the Americas. In 2023, the Peer Support Network grew to include over 70 peers across 26 countries, speaking 34 languages.

While not professional counselors, these fellow staff members have been trained in active listening and self-care by CiC, a London-based mental health services company. The network provides an accessible and informal space for employees to share their concerns openly with their peers while serving as a bridge to professional counselors.

The Peer Support Network has been instrumental in nurturing a culture of listening and mutual support across Reuters global workforce. To ensure sustainability, CiC provides 24/7 support to the Peer Support Network. In recent years, Reuters has recognized the impact of this initiative and acknowledged that the Peer Support Network has created opportunities for all employees to feel more heard and supported.

3. Leadership Involvement

Leadership involvement is crucial in enhancing active listening. When leaders prioritize and role model active listening, they set a powerful example that cascades through all levels of the organization. Their involvement reinforces the importance of truly listening and understanding others, encouraging teams to engage in more meaningful and effective communication. Without this commitment, employees may feel demotivated and disengaged and teams may begin to avoid raising critical issues altogether, leading to missed new opportunities or unresolved conflicts. Hence, leadership involvement is critical in building a strong listening culture to strengthen connections and collaborations across teams in an organization.

Nissan Group U.S., a leading automotive company, is an interesting example of how leadership involvement can enhance active listening. Between 2021 and 2023, the company introduced several initiatives aimed at prioritizing active listening through the involvement of its leadership. Central to Nissan's approach was its open-door culture, designed to encourage employees to communicate with leaders through various channels, including phone, text, email, and in-person meetings. This initiative was rooted in the company's belief that *"employees are truly the heart of the business,"* as emphasized by Jeremie Papin, Chairperson for Nissan Americas.

At the executive level, initiatives included monthly Management Information Exchange (MIE) sessions to provide leaders with practical tools for effective communication, including active listening. Senior leaders, including Papin, hosted "Ask Us Anything" sessions where they engaged directly with employees at various levels to hear their feedback and understand their perspectives. Regular town hall meetings further reinforced this approach, offering employees a platform to ask questions in an open forum. In addition, leaders and HR staff regularly walked the factory floors at Nissan's manufacturing sites to connect and listen to employees and address their concerns firsthand.

The impact of Nissan's commitment to active listening has been significant. According to Great Place to Work®, by 2023, Nissan achieved a 10-percentage point increase in employees expressing a desire to stay long-term compared to their first survey in 2021 and 83% of employees reported feeling more positively connected to their workplace and organization.

Element 2: Open Feedback Channels

Open feedback channels are rooted in active listening and allow employees to share their thoughts, concerns, and ideas without fear, creating a transparent and inclusive environment. The impact of open feedback channels can't be overstated. They empower employees by giving them a voice, and when employees know that their input matters, they become more engaged in their work and contribute more meaningfully to the organization's overall success. This is backed by research from Gallup in 2023, which found that companies with effective feedback systems see up to a 21% increase in profitability and higher engagement levels. When communication is a two-way process, employees develop a stronger sense of ownership and pride in their work, knowing that their ideas and inputs can lead to tangible changes and results.

To truly understand the impact of open feedback channels, we must talk about psychological safety. The concept of psychological safety was first introduced by Harvard professor Amy Edmondson in 1999. She described it as a shared belief that individuals can speak openly about any concerns or ideas they have, without fearing negative consequences like embarrassment, rejection, or punishment. In practical terms, psychological safety removes the barriers that might hold employees back from speaking up and they are more likely to engage in open dialogue, enhancing a listening culture where their input is seen as valuable rather than disruptive.

Today, psychological safety has become central to any organization that wants to grow and build an innovative culture centered around its people.

Research shows the significant benefits of open feedback channels. A 2016 study featured in the Harvard Business Review revealed that teams implementing consistent feedback mechanisms experienced a remarkable 25% boost in overall employee performance. Organizations that have these in place are likely to tackle challenges more effectively, leading to higher productivity and results.

To understand this further, let's take a closer look at **three key strategies** for effectively restoring open feedback channels in an organization's culture.

1. Feedback from All Levels

A critical step in creating a culture of open feedback channels is to clearly communicate its purpose and collect it effectively from all levels of the organization. When organizations do this and are transparent about feedback expectations, they create an environment where employees feel safe and empowered to share their thoughts openly.

Micron Technology in Singapore provides a compelling example of how collecting feedback from all levels can transform workplace cultures. Starting in 2019, Micron implemented employee surveys and listening sessions designed to capture a broad range of insights, including workplace experiences and employee well-being. One key initiative, the Engage! program, illustrates how Micron operationalizes this feedback. Conducted biannually, the Engage! surveys are designed to encourage open feedback across the organization. Leaders at Micron play a critical part in the seamless implementation of these surveys and in making sure that feedback is collected from all levels of the organization. The strong participation rate, with 95% of employees contributing to the October 2019 survey, shows the workforce's engagement and trust in the process. Following the survey, Micron takes concrete steps to address the feedback, with 80% of teams having tailored follow-up action plans implemented.

Building on this success, Micron's Voice program has since become the company's primary platform for collecting employee feedback and enhancing engagement. Featured in Micron's 2023 Sustainability Report, 89% of employees engaged through the Voice program shared feedback openly with over 160,000 written comments, demonstrating its feedback-rich culture. By incorporating open feedback channels such as Engage! and Voice into the organization, Micron has reinforced its commitment to listening to its employees, taking feedback from all levels, and continuously improving its workplace experiences.

2. *Ongoing Feedback*

Creating a culture of feedback involves actively and continuously giving and seeking input from employees. It allows organizations to identify potential issues early, celebrate successes, and create actionable pathways for growth and improvement for their employees. Without ongoing feedback, employees may feel uncertain about their performance and can lead to decreased engagement and productivity. This can create an environment where issues and frustrations fester unaddressed, potentially resulting in toxicity.

American Express, a U.S.-based multinational financial services corporation, serves as a great example of incorporating ongoing feedback into its culture. The company employs a comprehensive system of annual engagement surveys and frequent pulse surveys to continuously gather feedback from employees on how to improve the organization. For instance, the company's Open Forum, launched in 2007, allowed customers and employees to propose ideas and share insights directly with the leadership team. A 2024 update revealed how feedback collected through the Open Forum influenced product development and helped in refining platforms like Amex Pay based on the feedback received.

Beyond surveys, American Express makes actionable feedback a key part of its employee development strategy. Ben Lane, Vice President of the Colleague Experience Group, noted in 2024 that the company prioritizes "in-the-moment" feedback, enabling employees to receive immediate clarity on how to improve their work. This approach ensures that feedback is an ongoing process that supports continual growth and performance at American Express.

2. *Timely Action*

For open feedback channels to be truly effective, employees need to see that their feedback makes a difference. Organizations should regularly review feedback and openly communicate how feedback is being addressed or implemented. This helps create an environment where employees feel valued, knowing their contributions have a tangible impact on the organization. When feedback is not acted upon or employees feel their input is ignored, it can lead to a culture of silence. Research from Gartner in 2022 reinforces this, showing that companies that respond to employee feedback in a timely manner, experience a 30% boost in engagement within six months, proving that timely action on feedback is critical in keeping employees engaged and motivated.

We find Medtronic, a US-based leader in healthcare technology, and its approach to timely action on feedback to be a good example here. After employees expressed a need for more visible actions related to racial equity in late 2019, Medtronic launched the Global Day of Action for Racial Equity in July 2020. The event involved over 100,000 employees from various business units who attended educational sessions and community engagement activities to increase their awareness on racial issues in the organization and getting their commitment to address them.

In addition, in 2020, the organization achieved 100% gender pay equity and 99% pay equity for ethnically diverse employees in the U.K., addressing a critical concern raised by employees over the past few years. These efforts show Medtronic's commitment to timely action on employee feedback, and it garnered recognition as one of the World's Best Workplaces by Forbes magazine in 2022.

Element 3: Commitment to Inclusion

Inclusion connects both active listening and open feedback channels in a very succinct manner. It entails integrating the perspectives of employees from different backgrounds, roles, and experiences into the decision-making process. This helps organizations create an environment where employees feel genuinely empowered, valued, and more connected to the overall success of the organization. Forbes reported in 2023 that workplaces where employees are actively involved in decision-making processes see greater trust between teams and leadership. This trust encourages employees to be more open and candid with their feedback and helps drive effective collaboration across the organization.

An important benefit of inclusion is its potential to drive innovation. A 2023 report by Great Place To Work® emphasized that diverse teams are more innovative and by incorporating diverse voices in decision-making, organizations are better prepared to develop innovative solutions and tackle complex problems effectively.

As we explored neuroscience, we uncovered profound insights about how inclusion affects our brain function to process information. Research from the 2024 study "Mutual Inclusivity Improves Decision-Making by Smoothing Out Cognitive Conflict" explains that inclusion reduces a phenomenon called "mutual inhibition", which means that when we involve diverse perspectives in the decision-making process, the brain experiences less conflict, enabling it to process choices more clearly and efficiently.

These findings show that inclusion creates a neurologically supportive environment that enhances trust, drives innovation, and builds more connected teams.

To understand this better, let's take a closer look at **three key strategies** for effectively restoring inclusion in an organization's culture.

1. Transparency in Decision-Making

One key strategy for driving inclusion in an organization's culture is to ensure that there is transparency in decision-making, and employees see and understand how decisions are made, and what criteria are considered in reaching an outcome. This level of clarity and transparency helps reduce any perception of bias or favoritism, which can hinder the decision-making process.

Transparency includes openly communicating the roles and responsibilities of participants in every decision-making process. For instance, if a decision involves input from multiple departments, it should be clear how each department's feedback is taken and how the final decision is made based on that input. This approach ensures there is clarity and transparency in the process and reinforces the fact that employee contributions are meaningful.

IHG Hotels & Resorts, a British multinational hospitality company, offers a strong example of this. Established in 2003, IHG's governance framework emphasizes clarity and openness by clearly defining roles and responsibilities for key stakeholders across the organization. The Board of Directors, with support from committees like the Responsible Business Committee, regularly reviews and oversees decisions, especially in areas related to environmental, social, and governance (ESG) issues. Senior leaders are also actively involved from various departments, including Procurement, Human Resources, Legal, and Operations, are actively involved in these reviews, ensuring that decisions are shaped by a range of diverse perspectives and viewpoints. This multi-departmental approach for governance makes IHG's decision-making processes both transparent and inclusive.

In addition, a key part of IHG's commitment to transparency is its Code of Conduct (CoC). Introduced in 2007 and last updated in 2021, it sets out ethical standards and decision-making principles for employees at every level. The CoC is reviewed and approved annually by the Board, and this review process is openly communicated to all employees. In 2023, IHG also reported a 95% completion rate for its annual compliance training tied to the CoC, reflecting a strong testament to its transparent decision-making process, with employees fully aligned and committed to the organization's policies and ethical procedures.

2. Elevating Underrepresented Voices

Another strategy for building inclusion is actively seeking out and elevating the voices of underrepresented or marginalized groups within the organization. Traditional decision-making processes often unintentionally prioritize the perspectives of more dominant or vocal groups, potentially leaving other important voices unheard.

For an effective inclusive environment, it requires seeking feedback and involvement from underrepresented groups and ensuring that their contributions carry meaningful weight in the decision-making process.

Intel, the world's largest manufacturer of central processing units (CPUs) and semiconductors, headquartered in California, USA, serves as a remarkable example in this regard. The organization has implemented several initiatives aimed at amplifying inclusion across its workforce, with a strong emphasis on engaging underrepresented voices. Its comprehensive RISE strategy (Responsibility, Inclusivity, Sustainability, and Enabling) includes ambitious goals to enhance diversity within the company, specifically aiming to double the number of women and underrepresented minorities in senior leadership roles by 2030.

To reinforce its commitment, Intel has innovatively linked a portion of its executive compensation to diversity and inclusion metrics, ensuring leaders are held accountable for embedding inclusivity as a quantifiable objective within the corporate agenda. Intel's 2023-24 Corporate Responsibility Report highlights tangible progress, stating that by end of 2023, 25% of technical roles at Intel were held by women. Intel's strategy highlights the importance of elevating underrepresented voices in ways that are intentional and deeply aligned with its vision and strategy.

3. Regular Assessments

In addition to transparency and elevating underrepresented voices, conducting regular assessments can be yet another strategy for driving inclusion in a listening culture. These assessments involve a thorough examination of who participates in key decisions, how effectively diverse perspectives are included, and whether certain groups are consistently underrepresented or overlooked. Over time, assessments like these shed light on patterns that may be difficult to spot in day-to-day operations but have a significant impact on organizational inclusivity and overall effectiveness.

Zuellig Pharma, a leading integrated healthcare solutions company based in the Philippines and operating across 16 markets in the Asia Pacific (APAC), recognized the importance of this strategy. In 2021, Zuellig Pharma partnered with the Business for Social Responsibility (BSR) to conduct a comprehensive inclusivity assessment designed to evaluate the reach and impact of their inclusion initiatives and identify gaps in policies, procedures, and governance. The assessment was thorough, asking for feedback from senior leaders and employees, complemented by an employment perceptions survey to capture detailed insights into employee experiences and concerns.

The findings revealed that while Zuellig Pharma was in the early stages of its inclusion journey, it already had a strong foundation to build upon.

The audit identified key areas for improvement, such as gender pay equity, cross-generational exchange, and mental health and wellness.

Following the assessment, Zuellig Pharma took proactive steps to address the findings and formed a core committee to address some of the key areas. It launched initiatives to focus on gender pay equity, created forums to discuss ways for different generations to work better together, and set up platforms to address issues of mental health in the workplace. Some of the results of these actions were humbling. The average gender pay gap at the company was lowered to 0.16% compared to the global average of 20%.

Through assessments such as these and through actively listening to its employees, Zuellig Pharma took actionable steps to create a better inclusive culture within the organization. Like Zuellig Pharma, there are many organizations that are on similar journeys or are doing well in this area. And no matter what happens with Diversity, Equity and Inclusion (DEI) in the future, what we know is that inclusion matters and doing regular assessments in this area is still highly recommended.

***

Over the course of this chapter, we've broken down what it takes to create and sustain a listening culture. By implementing some of the strategies and examples we've shared, you can begin laying a strong foundation for meaningful cultural restoration.

To tie it all together, let's revisit everything through a micro case study that shows how it all comes together in a thriving, restored organization.

Amplifying Voices:
Netflix's Commitment to Listening

In exploring the impact of a listening culture, it's fitting to look at Netflix- an organization that upholds this approach through its policies and practices. Netflix's culture, rooted in principles of open communication and honesty, focuses on active listening, open feedback channels, and inclusive decision-making. Netflix encourages all employees to share their opinions openly about shaping the company's future and collectively driving its success.

Active Listening

Netflix has deliberately structured its organizational culture to prioritize active listening. A core element of this is its emphasis on honesty, a principle central to its widely recognized Culture Memo, which was updated in 2023. The memo outlines how employees are strongly encouraged to engage in candid conversations with peers, supervisors, and leaders within the organization.

Leadership involvement plays a key role in sustaining Netflix's active listening culture. As shared in its Culture Memo, leaders are trained to follow a "context over control" approach, equipping employees with relevant information to make informed decisions rather than micromanaging their work. Additionally, senior executives actively participate in regular feedback sessions and informal discussions, listening to employee concerns and workplace dynamics firsthand. This level of involvement reinforces leadership's commitment to active listening, demonstrating that employees' voices contribute meaningfully to the organization's decision-making.

Open Feedback Channels

Netflix also distinguishes itself through its commitment to open feedback channels. The company moved away from traditional annual performance reviews in 2014, adopting a 360-degree feedback system that engages employees at all levels. This system encourages feedback from peers, subordinates, and managers alike, initially adopting anonymity for employees. As the culture of listening matured and people became more open, Netflix evolved this process to include signed feedback and eventually face-to-face interactions, which promoted transparency and mutual dialogue.

The organization emphasizes frequent and timely feedback rather than relegating it to an annual event, maintaining relevance and immediacy in employee development. Netflix employs the "Stop, Start, Continue" model, which provides clear, actionable guidance on behaviors employees should adjust. This method ensures that feedback directly contributes to personal and professional growth.

Additionally, Netflix places a strong emphasis on peer reviews, enriching the feedback channels further. Employees are expected to provide feedback not just to their direct reports or managers but also to colleagues across different teams. Reed Hastings, CEO of Netflix, notes that it is common for employees to review upwards of ten colleagues during each cycle, with some providing feedback to as many as thirty or forty peers.

Commitment to Inclusion

Netflix's approach to decision-making is grounded in inclusion and transparency, ensuring that every member of the organization, from board members to frontline employees, has access to the same comprehensive data. Highlighted in a 2023 Stanford Graduate School of Business study, this method involves structuring board presentations as online memos linked directly to shared systems that are accessible openly to all employees.

Netflix's focus on inclusion is further enhanced through its partnership with the USC Annenberg Inclusion Initiative. In 2023, this collaboration resulted in a detailed report analyzing underrepresented voices within Netflix's content and workforce. The study noted advancements in the representation of diverse directors, writers, and producers and pointed out areas needing improvement, such as enhancing Latin representation. These efforts are part of a comprehensive strategy to ensure that the insights and perspectives of a diverse workforce guide Netflix's content creation and corporate decisions, reinforcing a culture of listening and inclusion across the organization.

Reflective Assessment

Petal 2: Listening Culture

After reading the chapter, what is your current assessment of your organization's culture?

1. Active Listening

What initiatives or programs do you have in place to ensure your employees are listened to and heard?

....

....

....

What are some areas that you still see need improvement?

....

....

....

2. Open Feedback Channels

How has your organization fostered a psychologically safe environment for collecting feedback?

....

....

....

What are some challenges you see in this regard and how do you plan to address them?

....

....

....

3. *Commitment to Inclusion*

How often do you include diverse perspectives and dissenting opinions before making decisions?

....

....

....

In what ways can you enhance this further?

....

....

....

Chapter 5

Petal Three: Ownership Culture

Think back to a time when you worked on a project that truly felt like it was yours, not just something assigned to you but something you deeply cared about. Maybe it was a report you worked tirelessly on, or a solution you championed from start to finish. The work mattered, and because of that, you felt energized and focused, knowing your contributions had significance. On the flip side, there are days when work felt purely transactional and discouraging, leaving you wondering if your efforts made any impact at all.

When we peel back the layers of these experiences, we find that taking ownership changes the way we work. When people feel a sense of ownership, when their tasks align with their values and purpose, it shifts how they approach their responsibilities. Suddenly, effort becomes seamless, motivation deepens, and accountability flows intuitively. It's not about being told what to do; it's about wanting to do it because you believe in it.

An Ownership culture builds on this truth and offers organizations a way to channel individual commitment into collective success. This is essential for any organization striving to restore itself fully to tackle complex challenges in today's increasingly volatile environment.

Once defined as VUCA- volatile, uncertain, complex, and ambiguous- the world of work has evolved yet again. VUCA was a lens to understand instability, but now it's shifted to BANI- brittle, anxious, non-linear, and incomprehensible- reflecting the heightened fragility and unpredictability of the current environment.

Traditional top-down approaches that once symbolized efficiency are at times proving ill-equipped to manage this volatility and the accelerating pace of change. The pandemic exposed the limitations of these setups and revealed the need for decentralized decision-making and empowerment.

This is where an ownership culture proves invaluable. It equips organizations to be agile and adaptive. Employees who feel like co-owners are more likely to go above and beyond in their work, respond swiftly to change and achieve breakthrough results.

To understand why this approach is so effective, we took a closer look at the psychology behind an ownership culture. It led us to Psychological Ownership theory, which offers insights into how people develop a deep sense of possession over their work.

The 2001 study *"Toward a Theory of Psychological Ownership in Organizations"* by Pierce et al. expanded on this foundational idea by identifying three distinct pathways through which psychological ownership develops. First, gaining control over a target- whether it's a role, task, or project- gives individuals a sense of authority and influence. Second, developing intimate knowledge of that target deepens their connection to it. And third, investing personal effort creates an emotional and intellectual attachment, transforming the target into something they care about and want to protect and enhance further.

In the workplace, this 'Psychological Ownership' is the spark that makes employees feel truly responsible for their work. It bridges the gap between "doing a role" and "owning a role." This sense of ownership further helps in aligning personal success with organizational success. People in an ownership culture are more likely to take initiative to solve problems, collaborate with colleagues to achieve shared goals, and actively contribute to business results. When employees feel that their contributions are integral to the organization's success, the organization starts to feel like an extension of themselves. This alignment builds stronger accountability and encourages behaviors that benefit both the individual and the organization.

Ownership Culture within the FLOWER framework™

An ownership culture drives intrinsic motivation to work on initiatives that feel meaningful, enhancing a fulfilling culture. A sense of ownership also empowers individuals through transparent communication, trust and inclusion, all key aspects of a listening culture.

In a well-being culture, a sense of ownership contributes to positive mental health and job satisfaction. An ownership culture also fuels an enterprising culture by inspiring innovation and encouraging employees to take risks. Within a results-based culture, ownership helps individuals take personal accountability to achieve results and drive collective success for the organization.

Through insights gained from our interviews with various leaders and a deep dive into research, we've identified three essential elements for building an ownership culture:

➢ **Empowerment**
➢ **Shared goals**
➢ **Transparent communication**

Let's delve into each of these elements in depth.

Element 1: Empowerment

Empowerment in the workplace springs from trust and autonomy, offering each person the space to shape their work and influence outcomes directly. This turns everyday tasks into opportunities for significant personal growth. We've seen this come to life in the stories people have shared with us. One memorable story involved a team member leading a major client presentation for the first time. They admitted feeling nervous, even overwhelmed, but what struck them most was the trust their manager showed. *"Knowing they had confidence in me and empowered me, changed everything"* they shared. *"I wanted to deliver something meaningful- not because I had to, but because I felt supported and it mattered."*

But empowerment is not just a tool for driving performance. It's a powerful antidote to disengagement, a persistent issue in many workplaces today. When employees are included in decision-making and encouraged to share their ideas, they feel valued and connected to the organization's mission. O.C. Tanner's 2024 Global Culture Report reveals that when employees have a say in organizational changes, they are significantly more likely to feel motivated to do their best. Specifically, they are eight times more likely to view their workplace as people-centric and five times more likely to feel part of a supportive community.

To support this, the 2017 meta-analysis research by Allan Lee, Sara Willis, and Amy Wei Tian, published in the Journal of Organizational Behavior, examined empowerment across 105 studies involving over 30,000 employees from 30 countries. The findings showed that employees who viewed their leaders as empowering, experienced greater autonomy and found deeper meaning in their work. This sense of empowerment also fueled creativity and enhanced trust. Employees trusted empowering leaders more, believing in their intentions and feeling confident with their decisions. This builds a virtuous positive cycle in an ownership culture, the foundational drivers being trust and empowerment.

To understand this further, let's take a closer look at **three key strategies** for effectively restoring empowerment in an organization's culture.

1. Delegate Authority

Delegating authority effectively requires giving employees autonomy to make critical decisions in their area of expertise and enhancing their sense of ownership over their work. When employees are trusted with this responsibility, they feel more motivated, leading to greater engagement and higher productivity. With support from the organization and access to training and mentorship, employees feel well-equipped and empowered to do their jobs. This support strengthens their sense of empowerment and helps mitigate any fear of failure they might encounter.

An example of this strategy can be seen at Bayer, a global life sciences company based in Germany. Bayer introduced a Dynamic Shared Ownership (DSO) model in 2024 to reduce hierarchies, eliminate bureaucracies, streamline structures, and accelerate decision-making processes across the organization. The DSO approach represents a radical departure from traditional top-down corporate structures at the company, creating an environment where every employee is elevated to be a co-creator and co-owner.

The DSO model enables decision-making to be delegated to employees, allowing them to act autonomously within their respective areas or teams. Bayer's aim with this initiative was to decentralize decision-making to improve response times and empower employees at all levels to make 95% of decisions that were previously made by management.

While the DSO initiative is still new in its implementation, early results have been promising. Teams are reportedly spending 30% more time with customers, cutting unnecessary bureaucracy and innovating faster. In the United States, Bayer has reclaimed 50,000 unproductive hours, while the Consumer Health Team in Southeast Asia has accelerated product launch timelines by 5–9 months, reducing internal process times by 60% and achieving a 30% increase in product value. These outcomes highlight the impact of delegating authority through the DSO model, and how it can significantly enhance efficiency and performance across Bayer's global operations.

2. Meaningful Contributions

Empowerment within an organization thrives when individuals make meaningful contributions. This approach focuses on creating a culture where ownership, collaboration, and creating a positive impact matter. However, a lack of meaningful contributions can negatively impact workplaces, where tasks can become mundane with an increased sense of frustration at times. Over time, this can create a toxic environment where employees feel their contributions don't matter and no matter what they do, they don't feel they add any value.

When we reflect further on this, Sebastian's participation in Camp Extraordinary 2024 (Camp X) in Singapore stands out as a relevant example. The camp was organized by Extra•Ordinary People (EPL), a registered charity whose aim is to form an inclusive society by supporting every child and person with special needs through community supported initiatives. Camp X was a three-day, two-night event designed to create a safe and inclusive environment for individuals with disabilities while giving their caregivers a much-needed break. What made this initiative exceptional was its entirely volunteer-led model, with many of the volunteers having disabilities themselves. This was a deliberate decision made by leadership, spearheaded by the CEO Ivan Chin, to create a space where everyone involved felt that their contributions were meaningful.

The camp's organizing committee, *Befrienders*, and other volunteers embodied empowerment at every level. Tasks were distributed equitably, communication was clear and respectful, and everyone was encouraged to share their ideas with the organizing committee. The Co-Chair of Camp X, a Special Olympics champion who was wheelchair-bound, exemplified how leadership transcends physical limitations when trust is enabled, and opportunities are provided to thrive. The camp participants, who had differing degrees of disabilities, solved challenges with creativity and collaborated seamlessly, resulting in an experience that was deeply rewarding for both the participants as well as Befrienders and volunteers.

Ivan provided the general objectives for the camp, embodying himself the theme of "Igniting Possibilities". The theme inspired everyone to think boldly of all the possibilities to make Singapore a more inclusive society. At every committee meeting, Ivan would continually remind everyone of the meaningful contributions they were making and how their efforts through Camp X created possibilities for all.

Similarly, Dr. Peggy Crowe's leadership in the MASTER Plan initiative, discussed previously under active listening, highlights the transformative impact of making meaningful contributions. Designed to aid new university students' transition into campus life, the program included workshops and social events aimed at building connections and life skills. Peggy's approach invigorated the initiative, and by empowering team members to embrace new challenges and giving them the freedom to innovate ideas to solve them, every team member felt that they made meaningful contributions.

3. Continuous Engagement

To build a strong sense of empowerment, it's important to create a work environment that involves continuous engagement with employees on organizational challenges or solutions. This involves creating a platform for employees to come together and discuss ways to bring about positive changes in the organization. When this is in place, employees stay motivated and continue to contribute positively to the organization's success.

Leaders play a critical role in driving this. When team members trust that their leaders are committed to engaging them in a transparent manner, they feel empowered and more inclined to fully commit and invest in their work. As a result of this, there is an increase in employee engagement and morale.

A great example of this is Tata Motors in India, which has facilitated continuous engagement to shape its "Culture Connect" program. Tata Motors' cultural transformation journey started in 2020 when their employees co-created the future strategic direction for the company. This involved continuous engagement with all their leaders to discuss which cultural aspects needed to be changed and which ones should be continued. Employees, along with their leaders, examined the cultural challenges together, creating an ownership mindset among them. They were able to share ideas and feedback openly with the leaders, and based on all the feedback collected, Tata Motors identified several key cultural principles such as boldness, agility, and collaboration to align with its strategic direction.

Furthermore, once these were established, they measured the impact of these cultural principles by collecting regular feedback from their employees. Throughout this process, Tata Motors maintained continuous engagement with its teams and employees. As of 2024 and the feedback collected so far, 120 new projects have been implemented at Tata Motors as a result of continuous engagement, including the introduction of Self-Directed Teams (SDTs) in operations and engineering, which promoted autonomy and empowerment within specific functions in the organization.

Tata Motors is a great example of how empowering employees through continuous engagement in shaping the future direction of a company, can lead to positive and impactful business outcomes.

Element 2: Shared Goals

While empowerment gives individuals the freedom to act with autonomy, shared goals create a sense of clarity and alignment for all employees on how they can, together, drive the overall success of the organization.

We've often heard how the absence of shared goals can fracture a workplace. Margaret, a professional from New Zealand who worked at a multinational corporation, shared her experience with us of feeling adrift in an organization that resembled "a collection of competing islands." Teams operated in silos, with little understanding of how their objectives connected to the organization's broader mission. *I didn't just feel disconnected from leadership, I felt disconnected from my own work,* Margaret reflected. This lack of shared goals within the organization hindered collaboration and created confusion, leaving employees disengaged and unmotivated.

In organizations that embrace shared goals, the environment is remarkably different. Teams align their efforts with a clear and unified purpose to solve problems together and celebrate the collective achievements of the team. This alignment strengthens open communication and mutual respect, creating an environment where collaboration thrives, and employees feel a renewed sense of pride and connection to their work. Knowing that their contributions are part of something larger, rekindles engagement and strengthens their commitment to the organization's success. In workplaces previously marked by dysfunction, distrust, or isolation, shared goals act as a unifying force, providing alignment and direction needed to rebuild and thrive.

Research highlights the importance of this. A 2013 HBR Analytic Services report on employee engagement revealed that organizations perform better when goals are clearly communicated at every level. It showed how top leaders play a pivotal role in articulating the broader mission, while middle managers transform these directives into actionable and relevant goals for their teams. This layered approach ensures that every employee has clarity on their goals, feels empowered to do their work, and knows what they need to do to drive the collective success for the organization.

Additionally, Patrick Lencioni's work on team performance sheds light on why shared goals matter so much. In his 2002 book, The Five Dysfunctions of a Team, Lencioni emphasizes that successful teams are defined not by individual accolades but by their commitment to shared objectives. He adds that when team members prioritize their personal success over the team's collective success, it affects and overshadows the organization's results.

To understand this further, let's take a closer look at **three key strategies** for effectively restoring shared goals in an organization's culture.

1. Co-Creation

One of the ways to establish shared goals is co-creating them. When employees actively participate in this process, they feel a stronger sense of ownership and alignment with the organization's broader vision. Research by Quantum Workplace, in their 2023 annual trends report, endorses this connection, revealing that employees engaged in co-creating goals with the organization's priorities, demonstrate significantly higher levels of workplace engagement.

United Overseas Bank (UOB), a leading Asian bank headquartered in Singapore, highlights how co-creating goals can drive better engagement and productivity. UOB was originally established as a Chinese bank with traditional Asian values dating back to 1935. Anchored in its Employee Value Proposition (EVP) of care, growth, and trust, UOB empowers employees to co-create goals that balance personal development ambitions with the bank's strategic objectives. Through workshops and open discussions, employees are given a platform to shape their roles within the organization's broader framework.

A standout initiative from UOB was the co-creation of a flexible remote work policy in 2022. Employees provided input on how to balance productivity and well-being, leading to the adoption of a two-day remote work policy for non-customer-facing roles. This policy was made permanent in July 2022, and it demonstrated the value of aligning UOB's goals with employee needs across the organization.

By integrating employee perspectives into its strategic direction, UOB showed courage in challenging traditional hierarchical ways of working, particularly hard to do in the Asian context. UOB's bold approach helped create an ownership culture within the organization, ensuring employees see the direct impact of their contributions on the organization's success.

2. Regular Communication

Building shared goals is not a one-time exercise; it requires regular communication to keep everyone involved and motivated. A key strategy for this alignment is creating platforms or tools that allow employees to stay updated on the organization's progress and help them understand how their efforts contribute to the organization's larger goals. When people see this happen, it reinforces their motivation and connection to the organization, creating a sense of ownership. However, the absence of such communication can create a sense of disconnection and misunderstanding among employees. Maintaining consistent messaging about the organization's mission, business goals, or even operational targets is a key step to ensure a sense of ownership.

One such organization that has successfully managed to use regular communication in fostering a cohesive and engaged workforce is H&M. Beginning as a single store in 1947 in Sweden, selling womenswear, it has since grown to operate over 4800 stores across 75 geographical markets and employing over 100,000 people.

H&M realized that there were a lot of different ways to communicate within the organization, but none connected employees seamlessly in a single, cohesive manner. To overcome this challenge, H&M deployed the One Team platform to create an inspiring and user-friendly way to help communicate with employees across different regions within the organization.

H&M also leveraged videos to engage employees through the One Team platform to share key organizational updates and progress of shared goals within teams in different regions. Besides the videos, the platform also featured employees sharing their team results and highlighting new campaign launches and success stories. Employees could also ask questions from anyone in the organization openly about any topics, updates or challenges.

As of 2024, the adoption rate of staff using the platform was 96%, and 86% of them were weekly active users. The One Team platform at H&M has managed to bridge the communication gap between employees in different regions and allowed them to engage with each other more regularly on their progress and goals, hence creating a better cohesion and engagement amongst them.

3. *Effective Collaboration*

Another key strategy for enhancing shared goals is through effective collaboration. This involves breaking down silos and creating an environment where individuals across various departments work together towards achieving common objectives. When employees are given opportunities to collaborate beyond their immediate teams, they gain an even broader perspective on the organization's mission and develop a stronger sense of ownership over collective outcomes.

LEGO, a global leader in toy manufacturing headquartered in Denmark, provides an excellent example of how effective collaboration can enhance an ownership culture. One of LEGO's most impactful initiatives was the Leadership Playground, introduced in 2019.

This initiative was designed to empower employees at different levels to align with LEGO's strategic goals while embodying the company's core values of creativity, curiosity, and bravery. It aimed to ensure that everyone at LEGO felt heard, valued, and respected, enabling them to make significant contributions to their teams. The Leadership Playground was built around three core behaviors inspired by how children play in a playground – "Be Brave" by doing the right thing, "Be Curious" by creating opportunities for new ideas, and "Be Focused" by prioritizing the organization's purpose and the commitment for actions aligned to that purpose.

To develop this initiative, LEGO formed a working group across functions, composed of 15 leaders from various departments who had never collaborated before. This group co-created the Leadership Playground to discuss LEGO's strategic goals and collaborate through shared goals to achieve them. The initiative was further enhanced by LEGO's adoption of Agile practices, which reorganized teams into multi-functional units. These units further encouraged collaboration between departments, working on iterative projects aligned with the company's strategic objectives.

LEGO's focus on shared goals and effective collaboration has also been a driving force behind its scalable growth strategy. In 2024, over 1,900 "playground builders" facilitated change across 29,000 employees globally. Over the period of five years, one in ten employees served in the role and successfully took LEGO's collaborative spirit into its rapid expansion efforts, thereby giving employees a deeper sense of ownership.

Element 3: Transparent Communication

For empowerment and shared goals to happen, transparent communication is a key factor connecting them. It ensures that employees are informed, valued, and connected to the larger organizational mission in an open manner. It's what bridges the gap between intention and impact, creating a workplace where the intention of communicating transparently creates the needed impact of a trusted and open workplace.

One of us worked in an environment where transparent communication was strikingly absent. Strategic decisions seemed to be finalized without informing others, leaving employees confused and frustrated. Major changes were announced abruptly, with no explanation or rationale provided. This lack of clarity and context wasn't just demoralizing; it created an environment of distrust. Over time, this eroded trust and made everyone hesitant to share their ideas openly, convinced that their input doesn't make a difference.

But this changed when some leaders decided to be open and transparent, and when they began holding weekly updates about the challenges we faced, explaining the rationale behind the decisions made, and sharing the progress everyone was making. Seeing leaders do this made a huge difference to morale. This openness rebuilt trust, boosted engagement, and employees collaborated more easily and effectively across the organization.

Research supports this broader impact of transparent communication. A 2024 SHRM report highlighted that 85% of employees feel more engaged when their leaders communicate transparently. The report also found that consistent feedback mechanisms, like weekly check-ins, correlate with a 15% lower turnover rate – a clear testament to how transparency in communication can strengthen employee retention.

Neuroscience also offers profound insights into the impact of transparent communication on our brain. The concept of predictive coding in the brain is vital in understanding how humans handle uncertainty. This neural process helps us predict future events based on past experiences. In a work environment, when communication is clear and predictable, it aligns with the brain's natural preference for stability, reducing the cognitive load on us. This allows us to focus more on the tasks that matter and less on dealing with ambiguity, leading to better morale and performance.

To understand this further, let's take a closer look at **three key strategies** for effectively restoring transparent communication in an organization's culture.

1. Authentic Leadership

Transparent communication starts with leaders who are authentic and who consistently demonstrate this through their actions and decisions. When leaders share information about challenges, successes, and key decisions openly, they create a foundation of trust and set the tone for clear and transparent communication throughout the organization.

Ho Kwon Ping, the Founder and Executive Chairman of Banyan Tree Holdings in Singapore, exemplifies this authentic leadership very well. For example, during the 2004 Indian Ocean tsunami, which devastated several Banyan Tree properties in Phuket, Ho Kwon Ping demonstrated transparency by openly addressing the crisis with employees. He shared the challenges faced by the company, including financial losses and operational disruptions, while also outlining a clear recovery plan to move forward.

By involving employees in discussions about rebuilding efforts and focusing on their ideas, he cultivated a sense of ownership in them. Also, his willingness to acknowledge personal flaws and vulnerabilities made him come across very authentic. In a 2024 interview at the launch of his book "Behind the Banyan", he highlighted how being transparent about his decisions and mistakes has allowed him to build stronger relationships with his team. He stated that *"authenticity is about acknowledging your flaws and not trying to project an image of perfection,"* a principle he applies both in his personal and professional life. Over the years, Ho Kwon Ping through his authentic leadership and transparent communication has transformed Banyan Tree into a globally recognized luxury hospitality brand, with its hundredth hotel set to open by the end of 2025.

2. *Ongoing Conversations*

Having ongoing conversations that are transparent is a powerful strategy that enhances empowerment and ownership within an organization. Open and ongoing conversations with employees on expectations, performance, and well-being can help build stronger trust and psychological safety with them.

However, when conversations are infrequent or only occurring during crises, it can make employees feel excluded and disconnected, leading to a breakdown in trust and morale. Ongoing conversations can involve any topic such as performance, culture building or discussions on business strategy. These conversations help build transparency, deepening a sense of ownership in employees and helping them better understand their impact on the business.

AbbVie, a global biopharmaceutical leader based in the U.S., demonstrates how ongoing conversations and transparent communication can shape a company's culture through its "Ways We Work" initiative, introduced in 2013 following its split from Abbott Laboratories. This initiative has five core pillars of employee behavior, one of which is "Clear and Courageous" communication.

To further focus on these behaviors, AbbVie launched the AbbVie Way Ambassador Program in 2013, shortly after its inception as an independent company. This program empowers employees to act as cultural ambassadors, communicating the "Ways We Work" behaviors throughout the organization. These ambassadors play a key role in reinforcing AbbVie's commitment to ongoing conversations aligned with its Ways We Work behaviors.

AbbVie also integrates continuous conversations into its performance management through the "Time-to-Talk" initiative, introduced in 2016. This initiative encourages managers to hold at least two structured discussions per year with their teams, focusing on the Ways We Work behaviors, and the learnings from it. All these transparent and open conversations at AbbVie strengthen connections between employees, making everyone feel more empowered and create a strong sense of ownership in them.

The impact of these efforts has been significant in the organization. In its 2023 ESG Action Report, AbbVie reported an 81% employee engagement score, which was well above industry benchmarks. This reflects AbbVie's success and commitment in enhancing transparent and ongoing communication within the organization.

3. *Leveraging Technology*

In today's interconnected world, technology has become indispensable in ensuring transparent communication, especially within organizations that operate across multiple locations and time zones. Digital platforms provide a seamless way to share updates, track progress, and engage employees in meaningful conversations. Real-time access to information ensures that everyone stays informed and connected, no matter where they are.

The Chalhoub Group, a leading luxury retailer in Dubai, UAE, shows how technology can improve transparent communication and build a sense of ownership across a dispersed workforce. With over 12,000 employees spread across 14 countries, 75% of whom are frontline workers, Chalhoub faced significant challenges in communicating effectively to all its employees across the organization. Recognizing the limitations of traditional intranet systems, the company adopted Beekeeper in 2020, a mobile-friendly communication tool hosted on Amazon Web Services, to ensure transparency and continuity in its internal communication channels.

By 2023, Beekeeper was fully integrated into Chalhoub's operations, providing a centralized platform for real-time organizational updates, tracking progress, and helping facilitate meaningful dialogue across teams. Its mobile-first design proved particularly effective for frontline employees, many of whom lacked access to conventional tools like email but could receive messages on their mobile, ensuring a sense of connection to the organization.

During a recent 2023 rollout of Chalhoub's sustainability efforts, outlined in its "Unity for Change" consortium, Beekeeper became a vital tool. It provided seamless and continuous dissemination of information across all levels of the organization. Chalhoub Group was able to leverage technology in connecting and communicating with its employees effectively, thus enhancing their sense of ownership with the organization. Sarah Cousin, Head of Internal Communications, said it aptly, *"The main reason we implemented Beekeeper was because we needed a way to communicate with our frontline employees, both top-down and bottom-up. We were way too disconnected from them. We could not continue that way."* Seeing how the staff can be connected now is a great way for them to feel a sense of ownership within the organization.

*****

Over the course of this chapter, we've broken down what it takes to create and sustain an ownership culture. By implementing some of the strategies and examples we've shared, you can begin laying a strong foundation for meaningful cultural restoration.

To tie it all together, let's revisit everything through a micro case study that shows how it all comes together in a thriving, restored organization.

Yara International:
A Model for Ownership Culture

Yara International, a Norwegian chemical organization headquartered in Oslo, has set a global benchmark for cultivating an ownership culture. As one of the world's leading producers of nitrogen-based fertilizers and industrial products, Yara operates with a clear vision that values responsibility and inclusivity across every level of its organization.

Empowerment

Empowerment is central to Yara's vision, guiding how the organization engages its employees to take initiative and make impactful contributions. A prime example of how Yara demonstrates its dedication to empowerment is by creating pathways for underrepresented groups to take on leadership roles. Programs like Black Leadership Development and Women in Agronomy are designed to break barriers and provide the tools and support needed for these groups to thrive in leadership positions. These initiatives are not just about representation; they are about giving individuals ownership to drive meaningful change. In doing so, Yara not only strengthens its internal workforce but also enriches the broader agricultural ecosystem with innovative thinking and fresh, diverse perspectives.

Leadership plays a critical role in embedding empowerment into Yara's culture. The organization has moved away from a rigid, rule-based approach, adopting a more flexible, value-driven philosophy. Regional management teams are now entrusted with the authority to lead compliance efforts, a shift that has enhanced communication and encouraged collaborative problem-solving across all levels.

Although not unique to Yara, the company has an employee share purchase program in Norway, which allows employees to acquire shares in the company. This initiative represents a commitment to giving employees a direct stake in Yara's success. By linking their efforts to the organization's achievements, it reinforces a sense of responsibility and ownership, inspiring employees to actively shape the organization's future.

Shared Goals

Shared goals are an integral part of Yara's identity, shaping the way the organization connects its work to a larger purpose. Yara's mission to feed the world responsibly while safeguarding the planet ties directly to its global priorities, including the United Nations' Sustainable Development Goals (SDGs). A notable example of this is Yara's focus on gender-equality, aligning with SDG 5, which promotes equal opportunities for leadership. The organization has set a clear target to have 40% of senior management positions filled by women by 2025.

Among several strategies to promote equal opportunities for leadership, Yara co-created a strategy with its employees for the Women in Agronomy Program which was launched in 2020. It involved employees co-creating goals to get diverse representation across the organization and strategizing ways to create mentoring and networking opportunities for them. As a result of this, over 60 women across all regions joined the program.

In addition, through constant communication of its Mission, Vision, and Values, Yara is also successful in integrating its position on inclusion into its core global processes such as recruitment and performance management. This integration aligns with the company's commitment to inclusion and is reflected in every aspect of its operations, guiding decisions and actions at every level. Co-creation and integrations such as these have helped create a strong sense of ownership with its employees and led to 81% high employee engagement index in 2023.

Transparent Communication

Transparent communication is a hallmark of Yara's operations, evident from how it interacts with the world outside and its day-to-day interactions with its staff. The organization is diligent about its sustainability efforts, annually publishing comprehensive reports that align with global standards like the GRI (Global Reporting Initiative) and SASB (Sustainability Accounting Standards Board). These reports are openly available to everyone, showing Yara's commitment to the transparency and the environment and society.

In its internal operations, Yara has centralized its HR processes across Europe with the aid of modern digital platforms like ServiceNow. This move has streamlined communication and made HR procedures more transparent, enhancing both efficiency and trust. Employees across regions now have equal access to information and support, which helps sustain transparent communication. Moreover, Yara regularly conducts employee surveys to gauge engagement and gather feedback. These surveys are more than just a tool for measurement; they are a critical part of Yara's strategy to keep communication channels open and active. The feedback received is integral to guiding the organization's decisions and strategies. High levels of engagement and positive feedback reported in these surveys reflect that employees feel strong a sense of ownership to the organization and are eager to contribute to the organization's growth and success.

Furthering its commitment to transparency, Yara also regularly shares its financial results with its stakeholders, reinforcing its strong position as an ethical organization.

Reflective Assessment

Petal 3: Ownership Culture

After reading the chapter, what is your current assessment of your organization's culture?

1. Empowerment

In what ways does your organization allow employees to make autonomous decisions in their daily work?

....

....

....

What are some challenges you see in this regard and how do you plan to address them?

....

....

....

2. Shared Goals

What tools or platforms does your organization use to connect and regularly communicate with all your employees across all levels?

....

....

....

What areas need further improvement?

....

....

....

3. Transparent Communication

How well does your organization show transparency in communication, policies and decision-making?

....

....

....

In what ways can you enhance this further?

....

....

....

Chapter 6

Petal Four: Well-being Culture

Not too long ago, when we found ourselves unraveling each petal of the FLOWER framework™ and reflecting on what truly makes the restoration efforts most meaningful, the aspect that kept coming up and was deeply personal to us was well-being.

A memory surfaced for us when we spoke to Aisyah, a tech professional from Dubai. She had been in a workplace that offered gym memberships, access to wellness programs, and even nutritional guidance. On the surface, it seemed like the organization cared a lot about well-being. Yet, as she spoke, it became clear that the focus was one-dimensional and only focused on the physical part. There was little acknowledgment of mental and emotional health. "I *had all the tools to stay physically fit*," Aisyah said, "*but I still felt drained, unseen, and unsupported.*" That gap made her realize how much more well-being needs to be.

Aisyah's words stayed with us, serving as a powerful reminder that well-being should extend far beyond physical health. It's about paying attention to a person holistically. Paying attention to their emotions, their interactions with others, and how they deal with stress and challenges.

When this concept is applied to organizations, it becomes even more profound. Great organizations take this idea and build it into the core of their culture, enabling physical, mental, and emotional health for every employee at every level.

The focus on employee well-being has never been more critical than now, especially in the context of the post-COVID era. The pandemic brought unprecedented challenges to people's health, leaving many employees grappling with increased stress, burnout, and uncertainty. According to the World Health Organization (WHO), in 2021 rates of anxiety and depression surged globally, with a 25% increase reported during the first year of the pandemic. Even as we've moved on, challenges related to well-being remain pressing. Hybrid work environments, economic pressures, rapid changes, and volatility push for an urgent need for organizations to adopt strategies that support the well-being of all employees.

A 2021 Gallup study revealed that employees who felt that their employers genuinely cared about their overall well-being were significantly more stable in their positions. Specifically, these employees were 69% less likely to be on the lookout for a new job, suggesting a deepened loyalty and satisfaction to their current workplace. In addition, according to Aon's 2022–2023 Global Well-being Survey, 83% of organizations reported having a well-being strategy in place, a significant rise from 55% in 2020. This shift highlights a broader acknowledgment that a well-being strategy is essential to the success of the organization.

Employees now look for workplaces that prioritize their well-being, and it is no longer about surface-level initiatives or checking boxes- it's about creating genuine support systems that acknowledge the complexities of modern work. Organizations that embrace this create a happier and engaged workplace, where employees give their best at work, leading to better performance and results for the organization.

Well-Being Culture within the FLOWER framework™

A well-being culture is intertwined with the other petals of the framework, ensuring an environment where employees thrive personally and professionally. In a fulfilling culture, well-being flourishes when employees engage in purpose-driven work and meaningful growth opportunities. A listening culture further supports well-being through open feedback channels and inclusive decision-making, reducing stress and ensuring psychological safety.

In an ownership culture, autonomy and transparency empower employees, reducing uncertainty and anxiety. An enterprising culture enhances well-being by encouraging innovation, keeping employees motivated and strengthening their sense of empowerment. Finally, in a results-based culture, well-being is reinforced through clear expectations and accountability, ensuring employees feel valued for their contributions and also connected to what drives organizational success.

Through insights gained from our interviews with various leaders and a deep dive into research, we've identified three essential elements for building a well-being culture:

- ➤ **Holistic Programs**
- ➤ **Work-Life Integration**
- ➤ **Supportive Environment**

Let's delve into each of these elements in depth.

Element 1: Holistic Programs

Just two decades ago, conversations about mental health in the workplace were rare and often dismissed as personal matters best handled outside of work. That perspective began to shift in 2001 when the World Health Organization's Mental Health Report emphasized the need to transform environments, including workplaces that influence mental health. Post the pandemic, as people returned to work following a period of collective trauma, the cracks in workplace well-being became undeniable. Today, the surge in absenteeism, quiet quitting, and disengagement highlights the cost of ignoring mental health and creates an opportunity for organizations to lead meaningful change. The Well-being at Work Summit 2024 in Singapore put these challenges into sharp focus, revealing that only 23% of employees are thriving at work, while 62% are either disengaged or quietly quitting.

Holistic well-being programs are fundamental to nurture a culture of well-being. These initiatives provide a comprehensive structure that supports employees' physical, mental, and emotional health. Without these programs in place, employees can face burnout and grapple with challenges that can affect their overall health and productivity in the long-term.

The economic rationale for this is also very compelling. Research from the World Health Organization published in The Lancet Psychiatry in 2016 reveals a staggering statistic: for every dollar invested in scaling up mental health programs, organizations see a four-dollar return in improved health and productivity.

Neuroscience also reveals the impact of well-being on our brain. Chronic stress, common in high-pressure work environments leads to elevated cortisol levels that can impair vital cognitive functions such as memory and decision-making. Over time, this stress-induced hormone can even cause structural changes in the brain, notably shrinking the hippocampus, a key area for learning and memory.

To counteract these effects, being involved in holistic well-being programs can significantly reduce cortisol levels for individuals and promote neuroplasticity, the brain's ability to form new neural connections or strengthen current ones. This brain's ability to adapt is crucial in building resilience, creativity, and managing change. By focusing on these programs, organizations can help employees not only manage stress but keep them more motivated and productive.

To understand this further, let's take a closer look at **3 key strategies** for effectively restoring holistic programs in an organization's culture.

1. *Organizational Alignment*

Holistic wellness programs are most effective when they align closely with the organization's strategy, ensuring that well-being is not treated as a standalone initiative but as a critical driver for organizational success. The 2023 CIPD Health and Well-being at Work Report highlighted that 76% of respondents were absent from work due to heavy workloads and management's expectations. However, around one-third of respondents reported that the organization's strategic focus on health and well-being initiatives had resulted in improved employee morale and engagement.

A strategic focus can help integrate wellness programs into the organization's operational framework and create platforms that provide employees with resources that are both accessible and directly tied to achieving personal and organizational success. The CIPD report further supports this approach, with the report suggesting that 78% of organizations are taking active steps to identify and reduce stress at work, and 53% of organizations now have a standalone well-being strategy.

Google's holistic approach to employee well-being is an example of how wellness programs can be aligned with an organization's strategy. The tech giant's organizational strategy centers on leveraging employee well-being as a core asset to build a productive, engaged, and agile workforce.

Google prioritizes holistic health through its Employee Assistance Program (EAP), which provides confidential counseling services, mental health support, and workplace accommodations for employees with disabilities. In addition, Google has on-site wellness centers which first started in 2010 and continued to expand in 2024. These centers offer services such as annual health check-ups, physical therapy, on-site pharmacies, etc., to help make healthcare services more accessible to all employees at work.

In addition, Google also has the gFit program, which supports physical health through fitness classes, mindfulness training, nutritional counseling, and on-site gyms. This program is part of Google's broader effort to promote a healthy lifestyle among all employees and is aligned to the American Heart Association (AHA) guidelines.

All these efforts reflect Google's commitment to supporting its employees holistically, which has been linked to a 37% increase in employee satisfaction according to a 2018 Forbes report. In 2021, Google enhanced its Employee Assistance Program by increasing the number of free mental health sessions to 35 per year for employees and their families and added 14 hours of virtual support for employees with caregiving responsibilities, showing its continued commitment to its well-being strategy.

2. Personalization

The next strategy in building holistic programs is through personalization. Tailored wellness programs recognize that each employee has unique health needs, preferences, and goals. This approach enhances the relevance of wellness initiatives and ensures that employees feel genuinely supported on their individual wellness journeys. A lack of personalization can make these programs irrelevant for some and weaken motivation for employees.

Swiggy, an online food ordering and delivery company based in Bangalore, India, has embraced personalization in its holistic wellness programs. The launch of a curated program during the pandemic in 2020, called 'Built Around You', aimed to support the holistic well-being of employees and their loved ones across four essential pillars: physical, mental, financial and legal. This program offered customized benefits tailored to the individual needs of employees at Swiggy. These included telephonic or video consultations with a range of specialists such as doctors, dietitians, psychologists, counselors, financial planners, and legal experts.

In a move that demonstrated a deep understanding of the interconnectedness of employee well-being with their personal lives,

Swiggy allowed employees to extend these benefits to three additional members of their choice, be it family or friends. For delivery partners and kitchen staff, the program was specifically tailored to their unique job roles; for example, delivery executives received access to a one-click helpline for medical consultations directly through their app. Employees were also able to enroll for a range of workshops related to any issues of health and well-being.

Girish Menon, Swiggy's HR Head, highlighted the thoughtful design of the program, stating it was *"built not just for them but built around them,"* underscoring the company's employee-first ethos. The impact of this initiative was both immediate and profound. Within six days of its introduction to delivery partners on April 1, 2020, the program saw over 2,000 sign-ups and over 1,000 consultations. When it was rolled out to the rest of the organization on April 6, over 120 employees signed up within the first two hours, showcasing the program's relevance and effectiveness.

In 2024, Swiggy introduced additional health initiatives, including Mobile Medical Units (MMUs) and teleconsultation services for its delivery partners under the "Built Around You" umbrella to further enhance the reach of its well-being programs.

3. *Continued Evaluation*

To ensure the success of holistic wellness programs within organizations, it requires a strategy grounded in continued evaluation. Regularly assessing wellness initiatives provides critical insights into their effectiveness, allowing organizations to make data-driven decisions that strengthen the initiatives. Continued evaluation also helps tie wellness initiatives to measurable outcomes such as turnover, absenteeism, and productivity. For instance, tracking metrics like reduced sick days, improved employee retention, and enhanced job performance provides tangible evidence of the impact of these programs.

Danone, a leading food and beverage company based in Paris, showcases this through its global program, Be Well, launched in 2023. Be Well is an expansion of the Dan'Cares program that began in 2009, originally designed to provide quality healthcare coverage to employees worldwide. The enhanced 2023 program is aligned to employees' needs and organizational goals and focuses on three key pillars: promoting healthy food choices, ensuring physical health and well-being, and supporting mental wellness.

To measure the effectiveness of its well-being programs, including Be Well, Danone actively monitors key metrics such as absenteeism rates and employee engagement scores. In 2023, Danone reported a low absenteeism rate of 2.9% and the organization achieved an engagement score of 84%, as noted in its 2023 Integrated Annual Report. In addition, Danone employs strong evaluation mechanisms, including the Danone People Survey (DPS). This annual survey gathers anonymous feedback and features a Well-being Index that measures stress levels, work-life quality, and overall satisfaction. In 2023, the participation for this survey reached 91%, with the global Well-being Index scoring 73%, which was above the Fast-Moving Consumer Goods industry norm of 70%.

Continued evaluation through these key metrics and surveys allows Danone to be fully connected to the evolving needs of its employees and helps refine its programs accordingly to ensure the sustained impact of all its wellness programs.

Element 2: Work-Life Integration

In today's fast-paced work environment, where remote work often blurs the boundaries between professional and personal lives, it's not about work life balance anymore but about integration. Achieving this integration in this new age of work has become a critical challenge for many.

Anna Sebastian Perayil's story brings a sobering perspective to this issue. As mentioned in the introduction, her time at Ernst & Young in India tragically highlighted the devastating impact of relentless work demands. The intense pressure to consistently meet high expectations took a catastrophic toll on her, exposing the serious risks employees face when organizations fail to prioritize their well-being. Her story serves as a powerful reminder that workplaces must focus beyond productivity and results. Employees need to feel valued and supported in their work, and conditions need to be created that allow for a healthy work-life integration.

A compelling study conducted in Oman by Al-Adawi S., et al. in 2022 explored the psychological effects of work-life imbalance on cognition. Participants who struggled with balancing their work and personal lives reported significant challenges with attention, concentration, learning, and memory. In addition, the American Psychological Association (APA) released verified data on workplace stress in its 2023 Work in America survey, highlighting the continued impact of stress in a post-COVID era. The survey revealed that 77% of U.S. workers experienced work-related stress and, as a result, 57% of workers reported negative health effects such as emotional exhaustion, reduced productivity, and burnout.

When employees feel overwhelmed and struggle in work-life integration, the effects can be both profound and far-reaching. This creates a vicious cycle: declining health leads to lower productivity, which then amplifies stress levels, and further impacts both employees and organizations. From a Neuroscience perspective, chronic stress affects the brain's neurochemical balance, reducing key neurotransmitters responsible for mood regulation and emotional stability. As a result, employees might experience heightened anxiety, depression, and other mental health challenges, making it difficult to break the cycle without support.

A healthy work-life integration is crucial for allowing the brain to recover and maintain cognitive function. Research such as the 2020 study published in Frontiers in Psychology by Loch et al., highlights how mental health recovery strategies like rest breaks can significantly enhance cognitive performance. The study found that rest periods after mentally fatiguing tasks boost focus, alertness, and balance, helping individuals return to baseline cognitive and emotional levels. As a result, when employees have the opportunity for genuine downtime, they return to work more engaged, productive, and innovative.

To understand this further, let's take a closer look at **three key strategies** for effectively restoring work-life integration for an organization's culture.

1. Flexibility

One common strategy for ensuring work-life integration is the adoption of flexible work schedules. Companies started adopting these more post the pandemic to offer employees the autonomy to tailor their work hours to better fit their personal lives, significantly reducing stress and increasing job satisfaction. Flexible work schedules might include staggered start and end times, compressed workweeks, or even part-time working arrangements.

An example of this strategy in action is seen at HSBC India. They have been implementing flexible work arrangements for some time now, much before COVID. At HSBC India, employees are given the autonomy to choose their working hours, provided they meet their productivity targets.

Reports suggest that HSBC's flexible scheduling has led to a significant boost in efficiency. In 2010, well before the pandemic, about 88% of its employees reported working more effectively since the adoption of flexible work policies, with no decline in performance noted for the rest of the year. This has still continued until recently, and according to HSBC's 2023 Interim Report, flexible working practices have become a significant draw for talent, with one-third of new hires citing flexibility as a key factor in their decision to join the organization.

Moreover, the support for flexible working hours is evident across various levels of leadership of the organization, particularly in its southern offices in India. Teams have adapted their schedules to better meet individual needs, such as coordinating with school timings or avoiding peak traffic hours. This localized adaptation highlights HSBC's commitment to being an employer of choice by evolving with the changing needs of its workforce and also serves as a compelling case for a 'Local for Local' approach, effectively demonstrating how strategies can be flexible and successfully adapted to meet local conditions and cultural nuances.

2. Leadership Behavior

Leadership Behavior is key in promoting successful work-life integration in any organization. One of the leaders who displays this best is Richard Branson. Branson says, *"It is not about work-life balance but rather work-life integration and harmony. I don't think of work as work and play as play.*

It's all living." He adds *"We all need to seek work-life integration and focus on boundaries instead of balance"*. He role models this himself all the time. When he's on vacation or on leave, he's disconnected from work as much as he can, and he encourages his staff to do the same. As work becomes more complicated today, it becomes even more important to schedule and establish boundaries to protect the personal aspects of our lives.

As organizations rethink work-life integration in the modern era, our work models also need to adapt to the fast-evolving needs of the workforce. Unlike traditional remote or hybrid models, Digital Nomadism has emerged as a new way to give employees even more autonomy in choosing where they work. This allows and encourages employees to perform at their best in settings where they feel most energized and engaged. This shift is particularly relevant for Millennials and Gen Z employees, who prioritize work-life integration by being open to working at any location. Virgin Group, under Branson, has also encouraged this. He says it is important that organizations give their employees as much flexibility to work around their personal lives. Virgin has embraced flexible working since 2013, and Branson operates on the foundation of trust. He says, *"We trust our employees to work wherever and whenever they like if they get their work done on time and at a high-quality level."*

3. Encouraging Time Off

A vital strategy for creating positive work-life integration is encouraging employees to take time off. While it may seem straightforward, creating a culture that genuinely supports rest and recovery is critical for maintaining focus and overall well-being. A lack of this can lead to an overwork culture and can create toxicity. In environments where taking time off is discouraged, either explicitly or implicitly, employees may fear negative consequences, such as being perceived as less committed when they do take time off.

Research shows the impact of taking time off. A 2013 report by the American Sociological Association, titled "Vacation, Collective Restoration, and Mental Health in a Population", found that people who take regular holidays experience a noticeable decline in psychological distress and performance. From an organization perspective, if we encourage employees to disconnect, we're truly investing in their mental health and overall performance.

Here we look at how Canva, a globally recognized graphic design platform headquartered in Sydney, Australia, has embraced this approach in remarkable ways. Canva actively encourages employees to take time off to recharge. In line with Australia's Right to Disconnect legislation introduced in September 2024, Canva ensures employees are not obligated to respond to work-related communications outside regular hours, helping them set clear boundaries between work and personal time.

Canva provides 20 days of vacation leave annually, supplemented by unique options like flex leave, offering five additional paid days each year for managing personal commitments. To celebrate milestones, employees reaching their five or ten year anniversaries receive extended paid leave along with a budget for an "Epic Experience," allowing them to rest, recharge, and celebrate. Canva also supports new parents with 18 weeks of fully paid parental leave from day one, regardless of gender or family structure, followed by one month of part-time hours at full-time pay to help ease their transition back to work. These comprehensive approaches have successfully improved employee satisfaction and strengthened Canva's culture of well-being. As a result, Canva was shortlisted for the Employee Well-being Initiative of the Year by the IEL Awards in 2024.

Element 3: Supportive Environment

As we explore the final element of a well-being culture, the importance of a supportive environment emerges as vital. A workplace that supports its employees fully in their well-being, can transform the employee experience, and increase engagement and productivity.

This ties back to what we mentioned in the preface, highlighting the strong impact a lack of a supportive environment can have. We saw how a once-thriving team could experience a decline in collaboration and morale under a new manager whose undermining behaviors created stress, diminished confidence, and strained relationships, ultimately driving talented individuals to leave.

These experiences bring to life what research has long shown: how people are treated at work defines the culture of the workplace itself. Studies such as Impact of Employees' Workplace Environment on Employees' Performance: A Multi-Mediation Model (2022) have empirically linked supportive environments to improved commitment, achievements, and overall performance. Conversely, the absence of a supportive work environment can lead to disengagement, high turnover, and a breakdown in trust, creating a ripple effect of negativity that hinders both individual and organizational growth.

From a neuroscience perspective, a supportive work environment directly influences the brain's neurochemical balance, encouraging the release of oxytocin, serotonin, and dopamine- neurotransmitters linked to trust, empathy, and collaboration. Oxytocin, often called the "bonding hormone," increases during moments of kindness and camaraderie, fostering a sense of belonging and mutual respect. This positive neurochemical response enables employees to share ideas freely, approach challenges creatively, and collaborate effectively.

Additionally, supportive workplaces enhance the function of the Default Mode Network (DMN), a critical brain network associated with creativity and introspection. In environments where employees feel valued and supported, the DMN balances focused attention with reflective thought, allowing for fresh perspectives and innovative solutions. However, stress and anxiety can overactivate the DMN, leading to rumination and diminished creativity. These neuroscience insights highlight the impact of a supportive environment on our brain and how it can boost efficiency and ensure a culture of collaboration and innovation.

To understand this further, let's take a closer look at **three key strategies** for effectively restoring a supportive environment in an organization's culture.

1. *Wellness Ambassadors*

Creating Ambassadors for well-being is one of the best ways to sustain a supportive environment. A Wellness Ambassador is a volunteer or chosen by their employer to promote healthy living amongst employees, while providing resources and supporting them in their individual wellness journeys.

Spotify, a Swedish audio streaming and media service provider, is a great example of how ambassadors can help in building a supportive work environment around employee well-being. Launched in August 2018, much before Covid, the Heart & Soul program is a mental health initiative built on a local ambassador program. The overarching aim is to create a safe and stigma-free environment where there's acceptance, awareness and support for mental health issues. Since launching Heart & Soul, Spotify has trained many of the ambassadors on Mental Health topics and provided employees with support through resources like the meditation app Headspace, All The Feels program, and an online self-care hub, all created by their ambassadors. The ambassadors also run seminars and workshops on mental health topics all year around for employees.

According to Spotify's 2022 Heart & Soul: Under the Spotlight Report, the ambassador network for the program grew from 15 members in 2018 to 75 members globally by 2022, significantly expanding its reach and impact. The 2023 Equity & Impact Report of the organization revealed that 83% of employees (Spotifiers) felt comfortable approaching their managers for support regarding mental health, while 88% agree that Spotify strongly advocates for employee well-being. In 2023, Spotify expanded its Heart & Soul offerings with new workshops led by managers during World Mental Health Day to reduce stigma on the topic and to encourage open discussions about mental health.

Through wellness ambassador programs, organizations like Spotify demonstrate that a workplace rooted in support for mental health issues can significantly increase psychological safety and improve the overall well-being of employees.

2. *Peer Support Networks*

Building peer support networks is essential in creating a supportive work environment. These networks enable employees to connect, collaborate, and share experiences openly, fostering a sense of community and belonging within the organization. By moving beyond traditional top-down approaches, peer support networks encourage grassroots connections, allowing employees to seek guidance and support from colleagues who have navigated similar challenges and experiences.

Kaiser Permanente, a leading American-based integrated healthcare provider, has taken a significant step toward enhancing employee well-being through its Peer Outreach Support Team (POST) program. Launched in June 2019 in Northern California, the POST program is now active in 10 hospitals across the region, with plans for further expansion. It serves as a prime example of how peer support networks can create a more supportive work environment, especially in high-pressure fields like healthcare.

The POST program was specifically designed to combat physician burnout and promote emotional well-being by creating a network where physicians can find support among peers facing similar professional challenges. By connecting physicians with colleagues who experience the same stressors, the program ensured that the support provided is both empathetic and relevant. Another key aspect of the POST program is its third-party referral system, which allows physicians to refer colleagues who may benefit from support but are reluctant to seek it out themselves. Dr. Molly L. Tolins, an emergency medicine physician and the founder of the POST program, highlights the significant impact of peer support networks in addressing "moral injury," the distress physicians feel when they cannot uphold their professional values due to systemic constraints. The program helps these physicians reach out to others if they need help, showing vulnerability and courage, but also letting others know that prioritizing their well-being is critical and important.

Since its inception, the POST program has shown remarkable results. A 2022 study published in PLOS ONE analyzed data from two hospitals where the program was active from June 2019 to May 2022. It reported that physicians involved in these peer support networks experienced improved well-being, a higher comfort level in discussing work-related emotions, and led to a positive influence on the overall departmental culture. Additionally, the survey results indicated that nearly 85% of participating physicians would recommend the program to other departments, underscoring its effectiveness and value.

3. *Digital Tools*

Another impactful strategy for building a supportive environment is through digital tools. Today, technology has made well-being resources more accessible and personalized. In this regard, Artificial Intelligence (AI) presents a great opportunity to address employees with burnout issues and help in proactively balancing work-life integration for employees. Generally, most organizations use reactive measures, such as performance reviews or employee surveys, to identify any burnout issues in employees. However, AI can help shift this perspective, using real-time data to detect early warning signs and help employees with timely interventions. For example, AI can help in analyzing work patterns of employees, such as email volume, frequency of meetings, and help in identifying individuals at risk of overwork.

This proactive approach is vital, as AI's ability to detect burnout early allows for interventions that can prevent turnover, which is often a result of prolonged stress and disengagement.

One such company that uses an AI tool to support its employees with their well-being is Microsoft. Developed in 2021, the company uses the "Viva Insights tool" that provides data-driven insights on well-being and personal recommendations to improve it for all its employees. It helps to identify potential burnout risks before employees reach a breaking point and helps them manage better work-life integration. For example, based on the data and insights, the tool recommends the employee to take breaks, guides in scheduling focus time, and helps in setting boundaries to prevent burnout. As a result, this helps in reducing their level of stress and being better organized, focused, and more productive.

The use of AI-powered digital tools like Microsoft's Viva Insights represents a significant leap forward in addressing employee well-being and preventing burnout. By leveraging real-time data analysis and personalized recommendations, these tools empower organizations to shift from reactive to proactive strategies in supporting their workforce. The ability to provide proactive tailored interventions, and promote better work-life integration not only enhances employee engagement and productivity but also contributes to a more supportive and sustainable work environment.

The future of workplace wellness lies in the strategic implementation of these AI-driven solutions, combined with a commitment to fostering a culture that values and prioritizes employee health and productivity.

***

Over the course of this chapter, we've broken down what it takes to enhance and sustain a well-being culture. By implementing some of the strategies and examples we've shared, you can begin laying a strong foundation for meaningful cultural restoration.

To tie it all together, let's revisit everything through a micro case study that shows how it all comes together in a thriving, restored organization.

Johnson & Johnson's Commitment to Employee Well-Being

Johnson & Johnson's Human Performance Institute (HPI) has pioneered innovative practices that redefine how organizations support employee well-being. Through its global reach and science-based methods, HPI addresses all aspects of physical, mental, and emotional health with its employees, and has set a new standard for cultivating a healthier and more energized workforce.

Holistic Programs

HPI's holistic programs for employees, particularly through its Corporate Athlete Resilience Program, launched in 2017, take a unique approach to stress management by helping individuals focus on managing their energy and learning to leverage stress for growth and performance.

The program includes an immersive 2.5-day experience led by trained coaches at offsite venues. It integrates multidisciplinary techniques such as cognitive behavioral therapy to address participants' thoughts, emotions, and behaviors. Participants engage in self-reflection, group discussions, and practical exercises to optimize energy levels and create actionable plans for sustained improvement.

Through the program, they also receive health insights from blood tests and personalized energy management plans. The program includes resources such as exercise guides, nutrition plans, and books like "The Power of Story" by Dr. Jim Loehr. The program has reached over 80,000 employees globally, with 15,000 participants completing it in 2023 alone. Reported outcomes include enhanced energy levels, improved healthy habits, better stress management, increased motivation, and higher productivity both professionally and personally. Specific statistics from participant feedback include 69% seeing improvement in their physical health, 71% managing their mental energy better, and 74% feeling more motivated in life.

Work-Life Integration

Recognizing the changing dynamics of modern work, Johnson & Johnson embraces the concept of work-life integration fully. The "J&J Flex" model, officially introduced in 2021, was part of its efforts to adapt to the evolving nature of work, particularly in response to the COVID-19 pandemic, and it remains ongoing as of 2025. This model allows eligible office-based employees to work remotely for up to two days per week while spending at least three days on-site. It also includes flexible work arrangements such as shorter work weeks, part-time schedules, job sharing, and remote work options. These policies aim to provide employees with greater flexibility to have a better work-life integration and help in reducing stress and overall well-being.

Additionally, Johnson & Johnson has been offering comprehensive paid leave benefits, with significant enhancements introduced over the past decade. Launched in 2023, the Caregiver Leave policy grants employees 10 days annually to care for immediate family members with critical illnesses or injuries. Enhanced in 2021, under the Bereavement Leave policy, employees can take up to 30 days annually following the loss of an immediate family member and 5 days for other family members. These initiatives show that Johnson & Johnson cares about creating a culture where employees stay healthy and maintain good work-life integration.

Creating a Supportive Environment

The Mental Health Diplomats program, an initiative launched in 2017 under Johnson & Johnson's Alliance for Diverse Abilities (ADA), aims to reduce stigma around mental health and equip employees with practical skills to support colleagues facing mental health challenges. The program has expanded globally and operates in over 30 countries, hosting more than 100 events annually on World Mental Health Day. The program uses the "LOVE" model (Listen, Observe, Validate, Encourage) to train employees to recognize mental health challenges and provide appropriate support to others. These efforts align with Johnson & Johnson's Credo, which emphasizes supporting the health and well-being of employees and helping them fulfil their family and other personal responsibilities fully.

Johnson & Johnson, through its HPI program, flexible work models, and a supportive environment, has prioritized employee well-being within the organization and has built a workforce that is more engaged, healthier, and resilient in the long term.

Reflective Assessment

Petal 4: Well-being Culture

After reading the chapter, what is your current assessment of your organization's culture?

1. Holistic Programs

What programs in your organization focus on holistic well-being?

....

....

....

What are some areas that you still see need improvement?

....

....

....

2. Work-Life Integration

What policies do you currently have in place that give flexible working options to your employees?

....

....

....

What are some additional steps that need to be taken to further enhance this?

....

....

....

3. *Supportive Environment*

In what ways are you incorporating digital tools to support your employee's well-being?

....

....

....

What are some challenges you see in this regard and how do you plan to address them?

....

....

....

Chapter 7

Petal Five: Enterprising Culture

As we continued progressing with our discussions on restoration, we found ourselves constantly inspired by the stories of organizations striving to restore their cultures. One such moment stood out during our discussion with a mid-sized hospitality company based in Australia. This organization embraced an approach that felt refreshingly dynamic and alive. They had given their employees the freedom to think boldly, experiment with new ideas, and test them in real-world scenarios.

A particularly intriguing and ongoing practice they shared was their Creative Sprints as part of their Quality Month, a structured yet flexible approach held twice a year to encourage innovation. Unlike traditional brainstorming sessions, these sprints in these months were designed as short, high-energy workshops where employees from different departments collaborated on challenges related to customer experience, operational efficiency, and service enhancement. Each sprint focused on a specific problem, and employees had the freedom to explore unconventional solutions, refine them in real-time, and receive immediate feedback. Leadership played an active role as enablers, offering insights, connecting employees to necessary resources, and championing new ideas.

What made this initiative unique was its consistency and regular implementation, making it an integral part of the organization's culture. Employees viewed these sprints as a valuable platform to innovate and experiment, without fearing failure. This ongoing commitment showed the firm's focus on building an enterprising culture, making innovation a part of its everyday operations.

An enterprising culture builds adaptability and resilience in its people, qualities that can help organizations in navigating through uncertainty and change. It transforms the workplace into a space full of possibilities and keeps employees engaged as active participants in achieving organizational success.

The importance of this is reinforced by research. A 2023 study conducted by APCO Worldwide surveyed over 500 senior executives from Fortune 500 companies, and sheds light on a telling pattern. While many leaders felt equipped to manage predictable situations, their confidence sharply dropped when faced with unexpected challenges. What set most resilient organizations apart was a shared trait: they had cultivated an enterprising culture. These organizations encouraged creativity, open dialogue, risk-taking, and the willingness to constantly reinvent and learn. This gave them agility to adapt and innovate during unpredictable and turbulent times.

Recent global challenges have made the importance of an enterprising culture more evident than ever. After COVID-19, businesses were forced to adapt at unprecedented speeds, with remote work becoming a necessity almost overnight. The companies that managed this change effectively had a culture where employees were entrusted to solving problems innovatively, adapting to change faster and navigating ambiguity successfully.

The rise of digital transformation adds a new perspective to this. In a world where technology is advancing at lightning speed, an enterprising culture helps organizations stay competitive by embracing a digital mindset to transform their cultures faster and more effectively.

And now, with AI becoming a key component of business operations, the stakes are even higher. AI offers immense opportunities for innovation and efficiency, but it also comes with significant risks and uncertainties. With innovation at its core, organizations that enable an enterprising culture are showing signs of adapting faster to AI-driven solutions and proactively addressing potential risks than organizations that don't have such cultures.

Enterprising Culture within the FLOWER framework™

An enterprising culture thrives when it works with the other petals, creating a dynamic and innovative environment. It naturally aligns with a fulfilling culture by providing employees opportunities to grow, take risks, and innovate with purpose.

Similarly, an enterprising culture flourishes when paired with a listening culture, as employees who feel listened to and heard are more likely to contribute to creative ideas and solutions. An enterprising culture also amplifies an ownership culture where employees embrace a mindset that the organization's success is their own, and they can transform results through proactive engagement and innovation.

In addition, an enterprising culture's connection to a well-being culture shows that when employees feel connected and supported in their health, it creates an environment where creativity and innovation can thrive. Lastly, the synergy between an enterprising and results-based culture is equally important. While a results-based culture emphasizes clear goals and accountability, an enterprising culture adds the creative edge that drives employees to innovate beyond just achieving results.

Through insights gained from our interviews with various leaders and a deep dive into research, we've identified three essential elements for building an enterprising culture:

➤ **Innovation Incentives**
➤ **Collaborative Spaces**
➤ **Continuous Learning**

Let's delve into each of these elements in depth.

Element 1: Innovation Incentives

When we spoke with Sara, the HR professional from the hospitality firm we mentioned earlier, her insights struck a chord with us. She described how her team came alive when their innovative ideas were noticed and incentivized. For them, it wasn't simply about monetary incentives but about the recognition, support, and trust they felt in being allowed to try something new. This conversation reminded us of a common thread we observed across organizations we spoke to: innovation incentives play a transformative role in cultivating an enterprising culture.

What makes these incentives effective is that they go beyond surface-level rewards. They create an environment where employees feel confident stepping into the unknown, exploring fresh ideas, and taking smart risks. It's about building a foundation where people know that their efforts, successes and failures alike are valued. This balance is crucial because, without it, the fear of failing can stifle creativity, leaving untapped potential within teams.

Research supports this as well. USC Professor Gerard Tellis, in his 2013 book "Unrelenting Innovation: How to Create a Culture for Market Dominance", found that an organization's internal culture, rather than factors like investment in R&D, is the key driver of innovation. Companies that create an environment for experimentation while embracing learning from failures tend to see a significant boost in engagement. Employees are more likely to bring their full selves to work when they know the organization encourages them to be innovative and their efforts will be recognized.

A survey by WorldatWork, in partnership with Dow Scott, Ph.D., a professor at Loyola University Chicago, further sheds light on this. The survey, done in 2022 with 523 organizations, found that 41% of organizations reward employees who contribute to innovation with bonuses or incentives, including 37% of organizations utilizing non-financial incentives. Of those, 84% reported these incentives to be effective or very effective.

From a neuroscience perspective, there are fascinating insights about the impact of creativity and problem-solving on our brain. A key discovery involves dopamine, a neurotransmitter linked to reward and motivation, which plays a crucial role in driving creativity. When dopamine is released in response to rewards, it sparks motivation, sharpens focus, and opens new ways of thinking. This process activates divergent thinking, the ability to generate multiple solutions for a single problem.

The brain's capacity for innovation is also tied to something called cognitive flexibility. This is the brain's ability to adapt to new information and switch between different ways of thinking. It's what allows us to reframe problems, see them from different angles, and come up with truly innovative solutions. When organizations offer incentives that encourage problem-solving and experimentation, it allows our brains to be cognitively flexible and makes us think more creatively.

To understand this further, let's take a closer look at **3 key strategies** for effectively restoring innovation incentives in an organization's culture.

1. Mixed Incentive Models

One powerful strategy in adopting innovation incentives is through mixed incentive models. For example, in a purely individual-based reward system, employees may feel pressured to compete rather than collaborate, leading to a cut-throat culture. On the other hand, an exclusively team-based reward system can leave individual contributors feeling overshadowed or unacknowledged at times, leading to frustration. This approach creates a dynamic where employees are valued and appreciated for their team efforts but not valued for their unique contributions. Hence, mixing incentive models must be implemented thoughtfully throughout the organization to ensure overall motivation and engagement.

Mars Inc., a global FMCG company headquartered in the United States, offers an inspiring example of how mixed incentive models can drive engagement and innovation in organizations. In 2013, Mars launched its "Make the Difference" Awards, a thoughtfully designed program that celebrated employees' individual contributions and collaborative successes. This included offering monetary rewards alongside public acknowledgment for innovative and collaborative ideas for individuals and teams, making sure all employees felt their unique efforts were valued and appreciated.

In its first few years, Mars received over 26,000 nominations for these awards, reflecting how deeply engaged employees felt in contributing to innovation. In 2022, the program continued to receive an impressive 13,000 nominations and culminated in a celebration in Washington, D.C., where 123 individuals and extraordinary teams from 23 countries were honored for 68 innovative projects.

This example shows when innovation incentives are structured to promote both individual and team efforts, organizations can unlock a deeper level of commitment and motivation from employees toward innovation.

2. External Partnerships

Enabling innovation incentives through external partnerships is yet another effective strategy to foster an enterprising culture. These partnerships guide and support the employees in refining their ideas, help them in overcoming their challenges, and push them to think innovatively about solutions.

One powerful example here is an initiative by Singapore Airlines (SIA) called KrisLab. Through KrisLab, SIA collaborates externally with research institutions, government agencies, start-ups, and educational institutions to bring in a wide range of knowledge and skills for employees. In working with external partners, SIA has developed and scaled new ideas faster, evidenced by its completion of nearly 340 prototypes and 40 proofs of concept since the launch of KrisLab in 2018.

KrisLab's further partnership with external partners like A*Star (the Singapore Government research arm) and the National University of Singapore (NUS) enabled it to leverage the use of Blockchain Technology and Artificial Intelligence to create KrisPay, the world's first airline loyalty digital wallet. In addition, these partnerships allowed SIA's designers to use Virtual Reality to "step on board" and explore or change future cabin design concepts faster, saving time and money for the organization. These collaborations exist even today and have enabled SIA to stay ahead and still maintain a competitive edge against other carriers. By providing innovation incentives in the form of external partnerships and engaging in impactful projects such as the ones mentioned, SIA has created a successful enterprising culture within the organization.

3. Gamification

The idea of engaging employees through gamification brings another aspect of innovation incentives to life, turning innovation into a shared experience that feels less like a task and more like a reward. By incorporating game-like features into daily work and operational processes, organizations can inspire creativity and collaboration.

Cisco Systems, Inc., a global leader in networking and IT solutions based in the United States, is an interesting example of how gamification can help drive innovation and enhance an enterprising culture. The Cisco Black Belt Academy was launched in 2019 to integrate game mechanics within the organization to create better engagement for its employees. In 2024, Cisco expanded the gamified features of the Black Belt Academy to address the challenges of maintaining learner engagement in its training programs. The Academy has elements like points, badges, leaderboards, customizable avatars, and themed storylines to immerse participants in the learning journey. One standout feature is the "Capture the Flag" mission, where participants test their knowledge of Cisco Systems in a competitive, game-like environment. Another feature is the "Escape Room" challenge, where participants assume the role of spaceship crew members stranded on an alien planet. To escape, they must apply their Cisco Security expertise to solve puzzles and gather critical repair components. These examples show how gamification can create incentives for employees and make learning exciting, while encouraging creative problem-solving within the organization through healthy competitions.

The impact of these gamified incentives at CISCO has been significant for the business. In 2024, partners with 60% or more of their employees certified through the Black Belt Academy experienced an average growth rate of 10% higher sales bookings compared to their peers without a similar certification. This example highlights how innovative incentives through gamification can create better engagement within organizations and can lead to improved business results.

Element 2: Collaborative Spaces

Establishing collaborative spaces within organizations is another key element of cultivating an enterprising culture. These spaces, whether physically structured within an office or facilitated virtually, are essential in enhancing innovation and boosting employee engagement. The design and functionality of these spaces needs to be intentional to promote effective collaboration across the organization.

Recent studies show the importance of these spaces. A Stanford study highlighted by Forbes in 2017 reveals that just the perception of working together on a task can increase performance significantly. Participants who were primed to act collaboratively on their tasks as compared to others who worked alone reported 64% higher engagement and lower fatigue levels. Another study by the Institute for Corporate Productivity (i4cp) and Prof. Edward Madden in the same year found that companies that promoted collaborative working were 5 times as likely to be performing higher.

Both these studies collectively affirm that having a collaborative space makes people more motivated toward their work and by creating such spaces, organizations can create an environment where individuals are more likely to share ideas, experiment with solutions, and build on each other's insights- all key drivers for innovation.

Neuroscience further highlights how these shared spaces can significantly influence team dynamics and performance. Studies from the Wharton Neuroscience Initiative, led by Michael Platt and Elizabeth Johnson and featured at the World Economic Forum in 2024, revealed that effective collaboration can synchronize brain patterns among team members. Often compared to the harmony of musicians in a jazz band, this phenomenon of inter-brain synchrony enhances cooperation, strengthens team performance, and creates endless possibilities for innovation. By understanding these neural networks and by intentionally designing spaces that promote such collaboration, people and results can thrive together in organizations.

These insights have profound implications for organizations aiming to build an enterprising culture. Whether through inspiring office layouts or virtual platforms, the environments we create shape how teams think, connect, and innovate. Harnessing the power of collaborative spaces offers organizations a unique advantage in unlocking their teams' full innovation potential.

To understand this further, let's take a closer look at **three key strategies** for effectively restoring collaborative spaces in an organization's culture.

1. *Creating Safe Spaces*

A vital strategy for building collaborative spaces is creating environments where everyone feels safe to share ideas and perspectives without fear of judgment. When employees trust that their voices will be valued, it leads to meaningful conversations that allow them to challenge each other openly and help in co-creating innovative solutions.

Without these safe spaces, organizations risk creating a culture where employees hesitate to speak up or share ideas, and this reluctance can result in missed opportunities for innovation and growth. Establishing these safe spaces is essential as they enable a culture of inclusion and collaboration.

When it comes to "safe space," many of us are familiar with the mental model of a safe space where we can have open and honest dialogue with people. This includes having a space where everyone can be authentic, and the conversation is held in confidence. But we don't talk much about the physical environment that we need to create for others to make them feel comfortable sharing their views and concerns openly.

This reminds us of the time when Nitin worked as a Regional Director at the Center for Creative Leadership in Singapore under Dr. Roland Smith, who was the Managing Director for APAC from 2013 to 2017.

Roland's office was a safe space for employees, where team members consistently had the freedom to test ideas and explore creative solutions without fear of repercussions. Right from the start, Roland trusted Nitin with his work and encouraged him fully to expand the organization's presence in the APAC region. We have heard many leaders saying that their "door is always open," and yet they tend to position themselves behind their desks and portray power over partnership. Nitin recalls that Roland was different and would not sit across in his office chair when meeting with team members but would rather sit with them in another designated area in his office. In one of those meetings, when Nitin didn't meet his targets that particular year, he shared it openly with Roland in his office, and Roland stood by Nitin, advocating for more time to achieve his results. This support strengthened Nitin's confidence in leading with an enterprising mindset, and as a result, the following year Nitin not just met his targets but exceeded them significantly.

One moment that stood out for Nitin was when Roland described Nitin as having "Ego Resilience," an ability to bounce back from setbacks while maintaining confidence and self-belief. This insight was empowering for Nitin, reinforcing the importance to him of learning from failures and quickly bouncing back to further develop and grow.

Roland created a safe space grounded in trust where sharing new ideas and challenging the status quo felt safe and encouraged. Team members were motivated to think creatively and aligned their efforts towards the mission of the organization. His often-repeated words, *"Remember to always create conditions where humans can flourish,"* left a lasting impact on everyone, including Nitin.

By creating a safe and collaborative space for everyone, Roland cultivated an enterprising culture where all individuals thrived, and the organization achieved impactful results and profitability.

2. Adaptability

Adaptability is yet another strategy in building effective collaborative spaces. These spaces should be able to easily adapt to different activities and working styles, offering employees the freedom to effortlessly transition between individual focus, group discussions, and creative brainstorming. The ability to shift between these modes of work encourages spontaneous interactions, which are often the source of breakthrough ideas.

Mayo Clinic, a globally renowned healthcare organization based in the United States, demonstrates how designing adaptable and multi-functional spaces can enhance an enterprising culture. A prime example is its "Condo" model, introduced around 2014, which has become a defining feature of Mayo Clinic with its flexibility and multi-functionality.

A condo is a group of investigators with a well-defined mission who agree to share research space and equipment to foster better collaboration and innovation. An investigator group can create a condo by approaching Mayo Clinic's research subcommittee, which is charged with creating the spaces that will accommodate these collaborations. For instance, the gastrointestinal condo (GI condo), one of the earliest implementations, has seen remarkable growth and success over the past decade with its innovation. According to Mayo Clinic, the GI condo has been instrumental in developing and refining minimally invasive endoscopic procedures. Since its inception, the endoscopic team within the GI condo, which performed about 1500 procedures annually, has helped reduce the need for surgery and shorten hospital stays, thereby lowering healthcare costs for Mayo Clinic. With the introduction of the GI Condo, 63.1% of patients achieved complete success without surgery.

The Condo Model adopted by Mayo Clinic demonstrates adaptability in collaborative spaces by allowing the reallocation of space based on the evolving needs for research projects. In addition to adaptability, grouping investigators from diverse fields enables the creation of more innovative ideas that might not have emerged in rigidly structured environments. The introduction of the Condo Model has allowed Mayo Clinic to be more innovative, strengthen collaboration across teams and contribute to a thriving enterprising culture.

3. *Leadership Vision*

Leadership Vision is key for turning collaborative spaces into hubs of innovation and creativity. By actively investing in these spaces, leaders create environments where employees feel confident sharing ideas, experimenting, and working effortlessly across teams. Leadership vision provides a clear roadmap for the organization, outlining where it is headed and how it plans to get there. Noah Ibrahim, once highlighted, "*As a leader, having a vision keeps you on course during stormy waters or unexpected setbacks.*" He goes on to add that leaders who have clarity of this purpose help motivate employees through challenges and give them clear directions to stay committed to long-term goals.

In this regard, Pixar's success in creating collaborative spaces through the leadership vision of Steve Jobs and Ed Catmull is an important example here. In 2000, Jobs initiated a major redesign of the Pixar headquarters. Jobs discarded the original plan for three separate buildings in favor of a single, expansive structure where animators, executives, and technical staff could all work together. Central to this design was an atrium, which housed meeting rooms, a cafeteria, coffee bars, and mailboxes, strategically placed to maximize cross-departmental interactions throughout the day.

As Ed Catmull noted, Jobs regarded employee interactions as the most critical function at Pixar. Leadership vision was fundamental to making this vision a reality. Jobs' hands-on approach to every detail of the building's design showed just how deeply he cared about building a space that supports and enhances a culture of innovation at Pixar. This vision, centered around a central atrium to encourage cross-departmental interactions, continues to influence Pixar's innovation and operations even today. It has helped Pixar tackle challenges successfully over the years and to produce groundbreaking work, such as 'Inside Out 2', which became the highest-grossing animated film of all time in 2024.

Element 3: Continuous Learning

The final component of an enterprising culture is continuous learning. This goes beyond being just a supportive practice to a strategic necessity for organizations, helping them stay innovative and competitive. When companies make continuous learning part of their culture, they create a space where employees feel motivated to grow, stay on top of industry trends, and adapt faster to a constantly changing business world. However, when a culture of continuous learning is absent, employees can often feel disengaged, and it can lead to quiet quitting.

Research highlights how significant continuous learning is for both employees and organizations in the present era. According to the World Economic Forum's (WEF) Future of Jobs Report 2023, nearly one-quarter of all jobs globally are projected to change by 2027, highlighting the urgent need for reskilling and upskilling initiatives. The report goes on to highlight that 75% of companies are looking to adopt new technologies in the next five years, with well over 86% of these companies expecting to incorporate digital platforms and apps into their operations. All this stresses the need for organizations to integrate continuous learning initiatives within their cultures to stay agile and competitive.

Continuous learning in organizations begins by cultivating a supportive learning environment that allows employees to appreciate different perspectives, explore new ideas, and have needed time for reflection. And it's important for organizations to implement concrete learning processes to ensure that knowledge is gathered, shared, and applied systematically. Research also shows a strong link between a culture of learning in organizations and job satisfaction. According to a 2023 SHRM survey, 68% of employees are less likely to consider leaving the organization when they have a positive organizational experience based on continuous learning. Organizations that prioritize a continuous learning culture also ensure that when employees do leave the organization, valuable knowledge isn't lost, but continues to inform the organization's progress. In addition, leadership plays a key role every step of the way. Together, all these help create an enterprising culture in organizations where continuous learning can truly drive innovation.

Neuroscience also offers valuable insights into why this is so effective. Studies published in Nature Reviews Neuroscience (2020) reveal that engaging in new learning experiences activates the prefrontal cortex, a part of the brain responsible for complex decision-making and creative thinking. This activation allows individuals to approach challenges with fresh perspectives and greater adaptability. In addition, learning agility, defined as the ability to learn, unlearn, and relearn quickly and apply new skills to adapt to changing situations, further strengthens the role of continuous learning.

What is equally important is the emotional engagement that continuous learning creates. When employees feel deeply connected to their work and see opportunities for continuous learning and growth, they are more likely to persevere through challenges and remain committed to the organization. This emotional connection creates an environment where creativity and innovation can flourish. Leaders must also champion continuous learning and set clear goals and expectations to successfully build it within the organization.

To understand this further, let's take a closer look at **three key strategies** for effectively restoring continuous learning in an organization's culture.

1. Knowledge-Sharing Platform

Creating a central knowledge-sharing platform gives all employees an opportunity where they can easily access resources, share new learnings and insights. The objective of such platforms is to make information flow seamlessly within the organization and ensure that all employees have what they need to develop and succeed.

Hindustan Unilever Limited (HUL), India's largest fast-moving consumer goods company, demonstrates how a knowledge-sharing platform can enable continuous learning. In 2016, HUL introduced "Chanakya," a data democratization tool as a knowledge platform that integrates internal and external data sources to provide employees with accurate and relevant information, and give them ready access to knowledge they need for effective problem-solving and decision-making.

Leaders at HUL also play a key role in making the platform effective. They use "Chanakya" to share their own insights and learnings engage through the platform, setting an example for others. This visible commitment reinforces the organization's commitment to learning and encourages employees to use the platform themselves in their own daily workflows and processes translating into tangible business results for the organization. For instance, HUL's digital transformation, driven by Chanakya's data-driven insights and focus on continuous learning, resulted in a 19% year-on-year increase in net profit in FY 2023-24, reaching approximately $350 million in Q3 FY24.

2. Cross-Functional Learning

Another impactful strategy for building continuous learning into an enterprising culture is encouraging cross-functional learning. By enabling employees to work on projects outside their usual roles or departments, organizations broaden their skill sets and help them gain new perspectives. Without such opportunities, siloed thinking can quickly emerge, where teams focus solely on their own objectives and lose sight of the bigger picture. This fragmentation can lead to misunderstandings, reduced collaboration, and even a toxic "us vs. them" mindset, with departments operating in isolation rather than as a cohesive unit. By integrating cross-functional learning, teams can break down these barriers and focus together on innovation and growth.

Philip Morris International (PMI), a U.S.-based multinational tobacco company, is an interesting example here. Since 2020, at PMI's Electronic Products Development Center (EPDC) in Hong Kong and Shenzhen, employees from various functions, including operations, supply chain, product design, legal, and procurement have all come together to collaborate on new product development initiatives. This has allowed employees to work collaboratively, while also enabling cross-functional learning from colleagues in different functions, creating a dynamic and enterprising culture within the organization.

What makes PMI's approach particularly effective is the way it integrates diverse workstreams into its projects. At EPDC, employees work collaboratively towards organizational shared goals, while gaining new insights into areas they might not have known before. Such experiences stretch employees beyond their comfort zone and enhance their ability to think innovatively and contribute positively to the organization's success.

In addition to these initiatives, PMI is planning to introduce an "Electronics Academy" in 2025, which will provide specialized training modules and innovative methodologies for employees involved in any new projects, further showing its commitment towards cross-functional learning. PMI's dedication to creating an enterprising culture in which employees feel valued, engaged, and supported in their learning and growth has helped them earn recognition as a Great Place To Work™ for the year 2023-24.

3. *Leveraging Artificial Intelligence (AI)*

To further strengthen a culture of continuous learning in an organization, leveraging AI can be very powerful. AI-driven tools can analyze employee performance, learning patterns, and recommend training tailored to individual needs. AI can also predict emerging skill requirements by analyzing industry trends and workforce data, enabling organizations to identify skill gaps and strategize for the future.

An organization we initially discussed, DBS Bank in Singapore, warrants a closer look when it comes to leveraging AI for continuous learning. One innovative initiative used at DBS is iGrow, an AI-enabled career development platform that was launched in 2023. iGrow helps employees to analyze and identify skills gaps and recommend specific development programs to bridge those gaps. Furthermore, the platform enables each employee to explore future career paths aligned to their skill sets. In 2023 alone, over 90% of DBS employees had access to AI tools to enhance their learning through technologies such as AI.

Beyond iGrow, DBS has also developed proprietary AI tools that reinforce its enterprising culture. ADA (Advancing DBS with AI) ensures centralized data governance, allowing employees to access high-quality, structured data that supports better decision-making and innovation. In addition, ALAN (AI protocol and knowledge repository) accelerates the deployment of reusable AI models across the organization, to enable efficiency, collaboration, and facilitate innovative problem-solving.

The use of these innovative tools not only saves costs for the organization but also creates an enterprising culture at DBS, where employees take full ownership of their own learning and growth and collaborate to drive the collective success of the organization.

***

Over the course of this chapter, we've broken down what it takes to enhance and sustain an enterprising culture. By implementing some of the strategies and examples we've shared, you can begin laying a strong foundation for meaningful cultural restoration.

To tie it all together, let's revisit everything through a micro case study that shows how it all comes together in a thriving, restored organization.

DHL Express: Building an Enterprising Culture

DHL Express, a global leader in logistics and express delivery, has created an enterprising workplace culture that thrives on innovation, collaboration, and continuous learning. This has helped the organization stay future-ready while ensuring a strong sense of engagement among its employees. Let's explore how DHL incorporates these core elements of an enterprising culture.

Innovation Incentives

At DHL Express, innovation is deeply embedded in the organization's culture. To encourage creative thinking and problem-solving, DHL has created multiple initiatives that incentivize and reward innovation at every level. A key example is the DHL Innovation Awards, launched in 2008 as part of DHL Innovation Day, an annual event that highlights groundbreaking ideas from employees, customers, scientists, and entrepreneurs. By giving employees a platform to showcase their innovations, DHL ensures that innovative thinking is actively incentivized. The impact of these awards is tangible, with many employee-driven innovations leading to real operational improvements.

For instance, in 2024, the Sorter Search System (SSS) innovation was developed by the DHL Express South Asia Hub team in Singapore and was recognized as part of DHL's strategy for employee-driven innovation. The SSS uses affordable off-the-shelf technology to proactively locate shipments that may have slipped under the hub's 305 carriers. It automates the checking process, taking only 2–5 minutes to set up and reduces shipment search times to just 10 minutes. The system has significantly enhanced operational efficiency and on time delivery rates for DHL.

Beyond awards, DHL has integrated gamification into its training programs to actively incentivize innovation within its culture. In 2024, DHL partnered with Kallidus, a leader in learning solutions, to launch Elemental Escapes, a gamified learning program designed to cultivate leadership skills while fostering a problem-solving mindset. By enabling skill development with innovation, Elemental Escapes encourages employees to think creatively, experiment with solutions, and apply innovative approaches to problem-solving.

The pilot phase alone engaged 25,000 employees and following its success, DHL scaled the program globally, making it available in 23 languages for all 600,000 employees. By embedding innovation-focused learning into everyday development, Elemental Escapes enables employees to actively contribute to DHL's enterprising culture.

Collaborative Spaces

DHL Express understands that collaborative spaces are essential in ensuring an enterprising culture. The organization has developed a variety of collaborative spaces and tools to ensure its employees can connect, innovate, and work together effectively, regardless of their location.

In 2019, DHL Consulting's office in Bonn, Germany, introduced a flexible workspace concept with 182 seating options spread across different zones. These spaces were tailored for silent work, team collaborations, and informal interactions. By creating an agile working environment, the Bonn office enhanced productivity and made it easier for employees to work together on projects or simply exchange ideas in a casual setting.

In the Asia Pacific region, DHL took collaboration to the next level with the launch of the Smart Connect platform in 2024. This platform revolutionized how teams communicate by enabling project collaboration, regular updates, and access to personalized services. These services include key HR resources like leave management and payroll information and streamlined onboarding support for new hires. Employees can also access customizable content through the platform allowing them to subscribe to specific updates or access local-language resources tailored to their needs.

Whether employees are in a warehouse, an office, or working remotely, Smart Connect has made it easier to share innovative ideas and help employees stay aligned with team and organizational goals.

Continuous Learning

At DHL Express, continuous learning is an essential part of helping employees grow and adapt in a fast-changing environment. The Certified International Specialist (CIS) program, introduced in 2010, is a vital example of DHL's commitment to employee growth. By tailoring training to specific job functions, CIS ensures that employees have the expertise and skills needed to excel in their roles. Over the years, the program has evolved to keep pace with industry shifts. In 2023, DHL introduced the CIS Digitalization module, designed to help employees develop a digital mindset by exploring opportunities in digital transformation while addressing concerns and challenges in this area. Employees are able to track their progress through a personalized DHL Passport, making learning a continuous and engaging process.

For managers and supervisors, DHL extends its learning culture through the Certified International Manager (CIM) program, introduced in 2013. This program focuses on continuous learning in leadership as a critical pillar of DHL's enterprising culture, equipping leaders with essential skills such as coaching, team motivation, and decision-making.

Beyond structured training programs, DHL encourages an enterprising culture by empowering employees to take control of their development. The Own Your Learning (OYL) initiative, launched in 2020, provides employees with personalized courses tailored to their career aspirations, ensuring they have access to the right resources to advance within the company. These initiatives reinforce DHL's belief that continuous learning should be proactive, flexible, accessible, and motivating for all employees.

Reflective Assessment

Petal 5: Enterprising Culture

After reading the chapter, what is your current assessment of your organization's culture?

1. Innovation Incentives

What innovation incentives have been most effective in driving motivation for your employees?

....

....

....

What are some areas that you still see need improvement?

....

....

....

2. Collaborative Spaces

To what extent are your collaborative spaces adaptable and how do they inspire creativity?

....

....

....

How can you enhance this further?

....

....

....

3. Continuous Learning

In what ways are you using technology or AI to drive better collaboration and learning across your organization?

....

....

....

What are some challenges you see in this regard and how do you plan to address them?

....

....

....

Chapter 8

Petal Six: Results-Based Culture

We've all been part of those moments when a single question disrupts the flow of a conversation: What are we trying to achieve here? It's often asked in frustration, in meetings where discussions wander without any objective, or in quiet one-on-ones where the lack of direction feels frustrating. The question, simple as it is, exposes a deeper challenge- lack of clarity on what results we're trying to achieve affects not just productivity but also employee morale.

In our discussions with leaders and in the course of our work, we've seen how this creates discomfort. Without a clear view of results, even the best efforts can feel directionless. People want to see their work build toward something meaningful, contributing to the overall success of the organization. But when this doesn't happen, priorities can shift unpredictably, and uncertainty builds up. Over time, this uncertainty wears people down, leaving them disengaged.

And yet, we've heard so many stories about what happens when this changes. When there's a clear shared understanding of what success and results look like, and there is alignment to measurable outcomes, it leads to a more motivated and engaged workforce.

A story that stands out in this regard is one shared with us by a project manager named Matthew, working at a global bank based in Tokyo. *"Before, we were always on the go, and it felt like we were just being busy for the sake of it,"* Matthew reflected. He spoke about his team's journey before and after his organization shifted its focus to results. *"Now, it's different. We know exactly what results we're going after and with this sense of clarity and direction from our leaders, we are more motivated and engaged to achieve our results. It's such a relief to work this way."*

This brings us to the next and final petal of the framework: Results-Based culture. At its core, this revolves around clarity and accountability. When people have clarity on their roles and are held accountable for their outcomes, frustration lessens, and there's a positive shift in performance.

But here's something we've learned the hard way through our own difficult experiences working in toxic workplaces. These organizations were intensely focused on results, and the push for outcomes. Without the balance of being human-centered, this created an environment that was anything but healthy or productive. The results did come in, but they came at a steep cost of burnout, fear, and disengagement.

This is why a truly effective results-based culture needs the support of some of the other cultures, like listening, ownership, and well-being.

When all of these come together, it creates an environment where people feel heard, empowered, and supported, and together, they can actively drive results that matter.

The importance of this is reflected in broader research. The PwC Global Culture Survey of 2021, which gathered insights from 3,200 workers across 40 countries, highlights the critical role culture plays in driving results. According to the survey, 69% of senior leaders see their organization's culture as a competitive edge, and in such organizations, all job roles are aligned to clear performance metrics and employees are held accountable every day for their performance.

In addition, another study conducted in 2021 by Truc Dinh Le and Yen Thi Tran, also explores how a results-oriented culture mediates the relationship between leadership and organizational performance in Vietnamese public service organizations. Surveying 205 senior and middle managers, as well as chief accountants, the researchers uncovered a compelling link. The findings showed that a results-oriented culture significantly enhances organizational performance through alignment of goals, clarity of expectations and built-in accountability. In summary, the study showed that Vietnam's public sector organizations that emphasize outcome-based goals and accountability, tend to achieve higher employee performance levels, resulting in achievement of better business results for the organization.

Results-Based Culture Within the FLOWER Framework™

In a *fulfilling culture*, linking individual efforts to clear outcomes gives employees a sense of purpose and meaning. Achievements become more rewarding, as recognition is tied to measurable growth and results. Similarly, in a *listening culture*, results-based practices give structure to feedback, turning employee input into improving individual and organizational performance.

In an *ownership culture*, clear performance metrics empower employees to take responsibility for their contributions with well-defined goals. In a *well-being culture*, clarity around roles and expectations reduces stress and helps employees navigate priorities and expectations without compromising productivity. Lastly, within an *enterprising culture*, results-based systems provide structure for innovation, linking creativity to strategic objectives and ensuring that continuous learning translates into tangible business outcomes.

Through insights gained from our interviews with various leaders and a deep dive into research, we've identified three essential elements for building a results-based culture:

➤ **Accountability Systems**
➤ **Clear Performance Metrics**
➤ **Performance Reviews**

Let's delve into each of these elements in depth.

Element 1: Accountability Systems

A key aspect of a results-based culture highlights the critical role accountability systems play in an organization. Accountability systems provide a structured way to set expectations, measure progress, and ensure that individuals and teams take responsibility for their work.

The importance of accountability is underscored by research from Partners In Leadership, which conducted the *Workplace Accountability Study* in 2015. The study revealed that 82% of respondents admitted that they have "limited to no" ability to hold others accountable successfully, and 91% ranked "improving the ability to hold others accountable in an effective way" as one of the key gaps in their development. This highlights the urgency of creating systems that empower employees and leaders to build constructive accountability without the fear of conflict or misunderstanding.

Building on this, Amy Edmondson's research on psychological safety and accountability offers invaluable insights. In her seminal 1999 paper, she introduced the concept of team psychological safety, describing it as a shared belief that a team feels safe to take interpersonal risks and are more likely to admit mistakes, learn from them, and improve their overall performance.

In a 2022 discussion, Amy Edmondson shed light on a common misunderstanding about psychological safety and accountability. Many people see these concepts as opposites and assume that focusing on one might undermine the other. However, Edmondson argues that psychological safety and accountability are deeply interconnected and essential for high-performance. Psychological safety creates an atmosphere where team members feel confident speaking up without fear of humiliation or punishment. When paired with accountability that focuses on growth, this environment becomes what Edmondson calls the "learning zone."

In this zone, team members feel safe taking risks and admitting mistakes while also feeling a sense of responsibility to meet performance standards and contribute to collective goals. In contrast, environments lacking this balance can fall into what Edmondson describes as the "anxiety zone" or the "comfort zone." The anxiety zone emerges when accountability is high, but psychological safety is low, leading to fear that stifles creativity and innovation. On the other hand, the comfort zone arises when psychological safety is high, but accountability is low, resulting in unmet performance expectations and complacency. The overall goal is to create a balanced environment where people feel both supported and challenged to perform at their best.

These insights remind us that accountability systems should be mindfully designed to inspire trust and engagement. When we looked at this from a neuroscience perspective, it became clear that accountability systems resonate deeply with the brain's natural preference for clarity and structure. The human brain craves predictability and actively works to avoid uncertainty, as ambiguity activates the limbic system, particularly the amygdala, which triggers stress responses. Research published in *SAGE Journals* (2016) also highlights a significant positive relationship between goal clarity- an integral aspect of accountability systems and organizational performance. When employees are given clear goals with accountability in place, they experience reduced cognitive strain, which allows them to focus more effectively and channel their energy towards achieving effective outcomes.

In addition, the interconnectedness of psychological safety and accountability can create an optimal environment for team success. With clarity of outcomes, psychological safety, and thoughtful implementation of accountability systems, people can thrive in their roles, and teams can drive significant growth for the organization.

To understand this further, let's take a closer look at **three key strategies** for effectively restoring accountability systems in an organization's culture.

1. Peer Accountability

One powerful approach for embedding accountability systems within an organization is through peer accountability. This strategy encourages employees to hold their peers accountable for their work and support each other's contributions. Instead of relying solely on managers, employees themselves hold each other accountable for their performance and support one another in meeting their target goals. Such peer-driven accountability is key in building high-trust and high-performing teams.

U.S.-based materials science company W. L. Gore & Associates demonstrates this approach through its distinctive use of peer accountability. The company operates on a lattice structure, replacing traditional hierarchies with a flexible web of interconnected teams. This structure enables associates (Gore's term for employees) to move fluidly between projects based on need and interest.

In this structure, accountability is distributed horizontally among peers rather than vertically. Each year, associates select 5–20 peers who have directly observed their work. These peers participate in a structured review process to rank and gauge who contributed more to the company's success. The resulting peer-evaluated rankings determine individual contribution scores, which are used to calibrate overall compensation for everyone.

In essence, employees report to their peers, not a single manager, creating strong incentives to deliver meaningful results that are visible and valued by teammates. This peer accountability model has helped

Gore sustain exceptionally low turnover rates of just 3–5%, compared to an industry average of around 20%. In 2024, 71% of employees said Gore was a great place to work, far surpassing the U.S. average of 57%. The company has also been featured on Fortune's "100 Best Companies to Work For" list every year since its inception, a distinction shared by only a dozen firms. By 2024, Gore achieved annual revenues exceeding $4.5 billion, showcasing the power of peer accountability in driving sustained business performance through an engaged, results-based culture.

2. Cross-Functional Accountability

Cross-Functional accountability aligns individuals' goals with the teams' broader objectives, ensuring that everyone feels responsible and accountable for achieving results. When team members understand that their contributions affect the group as a whole and they are accountable, collaboration becomes a seamless process.

Azbil Corporation, a Japanese company specializing in automation and sustainability solutions, provides a good example of this. In 2023, Azbil enforced cross-functional accountability with its Three-Tier Risk Management System as they realized that risk management needed to be integrated bottom-up as well as top-down. This system included all organizational levels working together to identify risks and implement mitigation plans to address them. Operational teams managed direct risks, support departments created mitigation strategies, and internal audits ensured compliance. The progress of the strategies they implemented was highlighted in their quarterly business reports to ensure progress was regularly monitored and that there was accountability for this at all levels of the organization. As a result of this system, the organization identified 119 risks and selected 16 as major risks to focus on in 2024.

To further enhance cross-functional accountability, the company established working groups to address challenges in achieving its Sustainable Development Goals (SDGs) and help in monitoring progress toward them. These groups ensured that all functions at Azbil work collaboratively to achieve their SDGs, leading to overall success for the organization.

The tangible impact of Azbil's cross-functional accountability strongly comes through in its performance. 89% of employees reported feeling strong satisfaction with their work and 59% cited personal growth in their jobs. Financially, these systems have supported three consecutive years of record consolidated performance, with net sales rising by 4.5% in 2023 to USD 1.93 billion. Recognizing some of these efforts and success, Azbil also achieved a Great Place To Work™ certification in 2024.

3. Role-Specific Accountability

A strong results-based culture also relies on role-specific accountability, ensuring that employees have clear, measurable responsibilities tied to their roles and strategic objectives. Rather than vague expectations, this approach creates a structured way to allow employees to track their progress within their roles and make role-driven decisions to successfully drive long-term success for the organization.

Hyundai Motor India, the Indian wing of the South Korean multinational automotive manufacturer Hyundai, implemented a role-specific accountability structure in 2023. As mentioned in their Annual Report of FY23, their journey began in 2022, when they embarked on their "reIMAGINATION" project which focused on Work, People and Workplace dimensions. This project involved restructuring all employee designations into "Responsibility Levels" and "Bands," tied to specific roles and measurable objectives. This project shifted the organization away from generalized job expectations toward a structured system where employees were evaluated based on clearly defined roles and contributions. Hyundai reassessed employee roles in alignment with market standards, and determined the right compensation for each role. Employees were then given titles and designations that reflected their roles in the broader context of the market.

Hyundai Motor India's strategy to move toward a role-based structure and accountability undoubtedly was a major contributing factor to a 27% increase in revenue in FY23, reaching $7 billion as compared to $5 billion in FY22. Additionally, domestic sales grew by 17.9%, reaching 500k units in FY23, while exports rose by 18.4%, totaling 100k units. These results contributed to Hyundai's sustained market leadership as the second-largest car manufacturer in India and earned it a Great Place To Work™ certification in 2023.

Element 2: Clear Performance Metrics

When we began exploring what truly drives a results-based culture, we conducted interviews with a mid-sized manufacturing company based in Manila, Philippines. During one of the interviews, a team leader expressed frustration about his constantly shifting deadlines. *"It's like shooting arrows at a target that keeps disappearing,"* he said. As we dug deeper, it became clear that the issue wasn't the deadline, it was a lack of clarity. The team didn't have clarity on how their performance was being measured or how they were held accountable. This experience reinforced in us that without clear performance metrics, even the most successful teams might struggle to deliver meaningful results.

Clear performance metrics are foundational in a results-based culture. They define success in concrete terms, cutting through ambiguity and providing a shared understanding of goals at every level of the organization. When everyone from individual contributors to team leaders have this clarity, it provides the organization with a structured roadmap to achieve their results.

But metrics don't just provide clarity; they also create accountability and transparency. Insights from McKinsey's 2023 report, Performance Management: Why Keeping Score Matters, illustrates how transformative clear metrics can be. The report highlights organizations using tools like production boards that align goals with everyday tasks in a transparent manner. These production boards provide a visual representation of employees' progress against organizational goals, ensuring that employees at every level can see the impact of their work and how it aligns with the organization's success. This kind of transparency builds trust and eliminates ambiguity, creating what McKinsey calls a *"single, verified version of the truth."*

Additional research sheds light on how clear performance metrics influence the organizational culture at a deeper level. A 2022 study by Gomez-Conde et al., published in Accounting & Finance, explored how high-quality metrics shape behaviors within teams. The findings show that when performance metrics are clear and well-defined, they enable better monitoring and accountability. In other words, performance metrics create an environment where teams can better hold each other accountable, learn from one another, and collaborate more effectively.

Upon further exploration, we found insights from neuroscience that explain why these metrics are so effective. As mentioned before, our brains are naturally inclined to seek clarity and dislike uncertainty. When we receive clear expectations on our goals and are measured by clear performance metrics, the prefrontal cortex, the brain's working memory, efficiently works to help us stay focused on achieving our goals.

To understand this further, let's take a closer look at **three key strategies** for effectively restoring clear performance metrics in an organization's culture.

1. Goal-Setting Frameworks

One of the most common ways to drive effective performance in a results-based culture is by embedding goal-setting frameworks like Objectives and Key Results (OKRs) and Key Performance Indicators (KPIs). These frameworks align day-to-day activities with broader organizational goals, creating a cohesive strategy for performance management. OKRs. focus on setting ambitious, qualitative objectives, while KPIs emphasize quantitative objectives that track ongoing performance against specific targets. Together, they create a synergy that fosters clarity, accountability, and a successful results-driven culture within an organization.

A compelling example that embraces this is Domino's Pizza, the U.S.-based multinational pizza restaurant chain. Since 2017, the company has utilized OKRs. and KPIs to tightly align individual and team goals with its overarching strategic objectives. For instance, one of Domino's key goals was to enhance customer satisfaction. By leveraging OKRs. to define clear objectives and KPIs to measure progress, the company introduced the "Pizza Tracker," a real-time order monitoring tool that improved both customer satisfaction and employee accountability.

The impact of this approach was transformative. Domino's saw a 25% increase in sales over two years, driven by its ability to connect OKRs. to innovation and operational excellence. Employees were motivated to prioritize customer satisfaction, leading to advancements such as the launch of "Pinpoint Delivery" in 2023, a groundbreaking feature enabling customers to receive deliveries at outdoor locations like parks or beaches.

In 2024, Domino's further refined its OKR framework by partnering with OKR Quickstart, a platform designed to streamline goal-setting processes. This collaboration emphasized simplifying objectives, aligning quarterly priorities with KPIs, and enabling teams to focus on high-impact initiatives. Matt Kershaw, Global Head of People Development, highlighted how this alignment helped maintain focus on delivering exceptional customer experiences at Domino's. The results of this strategic alignment were clear: Domino's achieved a 5.1% year-over-year revenue growth, reaching $1.08 billion by Q3 2024.

By combining the ambitious goal setting aspects of OKRs. with precise tracking capabilities of KPIs, organizations like Domino's demonstrate how these frameworks can foster a people-centered focus, and transform performance management into a powerful driver for growth and excellence.

2. Data Governance

Having clear performance metrics is essential, but their impact depends on the quality of the data behind them. Accurate, consistent, and reliable data form the backbone of any results-based culture, ensuring that all performance metrics accurately reflect progress and help in decision-making. Without strong data governance systems, organizations risk basing critical decisions on flawed information, leading to misaligned strategies and diminished trust.

An inspiring example of this can be seen at Celcom, one of Malaysia's leading telecom companies. As part of its digital transformation efforts in 2018, Celcom launched an enterprise-wide data governance program to address inconsistencies in its performance metrics and overall decision-making. The program focused on fostering a culture in which data integrity was non-negotiable.

The organization started by establishing a centralized data lake that unified data from all business units, eliminating duplication and streamlining access. In 2019, Celcom trained 52 "data governance champions" across various departments to embed accountability and awareness on data integrity. This human-centered approach through these champions played a key role in integrating governance practices into everyday workflows. To ensure buy-in at all levels, the organization also hosted a "Data Festival" in 2019, an initiative designed to celebrate the cultural shift towards data-driven decision-making. This initiative was instrumental in improving Celcom's data governance score from 30% in January 2019 to 95% in 2019.

In 2022, Celcom merged with another telecom Digi, making it the largest telecom operator in Malaysia. In 2023 and 2024, Celcom branded under CelcomDigi continued to build on its enterprise-wide data governance program. A major milestone for the organization was the successful implementation of Project Axon, which automated and streamlined data governance processes, enhancing both efficiency and accuracy. One of the key aspects of Project Axon was when it automated the process of compliance reporting to the Malaysian Communications and Multimedia Commission (MCMC). What previously required 150 man-hours of manual processing was reduced to just 5 hours, representing a 3000% improvement in efficiency, marking a significant achievement. Through its accurate processing and data governance practices across the organization, and initiatives like Project Axon and "data governance champions", Celcom was able to drive a successful results-based culture by building better trust among its stakeholders and employees.

3. *Leading and Lagging Indicators*

Another key approach for performance metrics involves balancing leading and lagging indicators. This provides organizations with a comprehensive view of performance by combining predictive insights with actual outcomes, ensuring a more cohesive understanding of progress and success.

Leading indicators are like signposts on a journey. They point toward potential outcomes by measuring the activities or behaviors that drive results. These might include metrics such as customer inquiries, employee training hours, or production efficiency rates. Lagging indicators, on the other hand, tell the story of what has already been achieved. Metrics like revenue, customer satisfaction scores, or project completion rates fall into this category. Together, these indicators form a dynamic system of measurement that informs both immediate actions and long-term strategies.

An example of an organization that effectively balances these metrics is Mizuho Financial Group in Japan, one of the country's largest financial institutions. Since 2016, Mizuho has integrated leading and lagging indicators into its operations to enhance decision-making and operational efficiency. The bank launched fintech laboratories in 2016 to drive open innovation through AI and big data solutions. This focus allowed Mizuho to track leading indicators such as customer engagement rates with its digital capabilities. In 2022, Mizuho seamlessly integrated a human-centered approach to performance metrics within their culture and introduced employee-led working groups to incorporate staff perspectives into its decision-making processes.

Since 2022, Mizuho has worked to embed these key performance metrics into its organizational culture as part of a broader corporate transformation strategy. These efforts include tracking financial performance through lagging indicators like net revenue and profitability while continuing to incorporate inclusion metrics into its decision-making processes. In fiscal year 2023, Mizuho achieved approximately USD 6.1 billion (a 6% increase from the previous year) in profits, aligning very closely with their targets for their 5-Year business strategy. The bank acknowledges that its success is closely attributed to some of these indicators in place.

Element 3: Regular Performance Reviews

Now that we've explored the importance of clear performance metrics and accountability systems, it's time to examine the last critical piece of a results-based culture: regular performance reviews. These reviews are structured opportunities to evaluate progress, refine goals, and align individual contributions with the organization's broader objectives. They are powerful tools for driving accountability, improving progress, and increase collaboration across the organization.

At their core, performance reviews provide a structure for meaningful dialogue between employees and their managers. They allow for a deep dive analysis into what's working, where the challenges lie, and how individual efforts can align better with the organization's goals. They're not just about identifying gaps; they're also about celebrating wins, identifying growth opportunities, and ensuring that everyone is fully aligned on what results they desire.

Performance reviews also play a key role in employee engagement and retention. In addition, recognizing individual contributions during these reviews sends a powerful message to employees that their work matters. According to a 2024 report by SHRM, organizations that integrate recognition into their review processes see a noticeable boost in morale and a reduction in turnover rates. When employees feel seen and valued for their work, they're more likely to stay committed to the organization's purpose and help in driving successful results.

Supporting this, Gallup's 2017 research titled "Re-Engineering Performance Management," reveals the tangible benefits of embedding regular feedback into performance reviews. According to their findings, companies that actively engage in ongoing performance discussions witness a notable increase in employee engagement- up to 14.9%. More so, these organizations see a significant rise in profitability, by as much as 21%. These statistics endorse the fact that regular performance reviews enhance employee satisfaction and drive better business outcomes and performance.

Insights from the NeuroLeadership Institute in 2022 reinforce this perspective. Traditional performance management systems, such as annual performance ratings, often activate a "threat state" in the brain for both employees and managers. This neurological response, triggered by fear of judgment or criticism, can impair cognitive functioning and derail developmental conversations. Recognizing these limitations, many organizations have transitioned to Continuous Performance Management (CPM), which emphasizes ongoing, meaningful conversations throughout the year instead of annual reviews and ratings.

In summary, these studies emphasize the immense value of structured, timely performance reviews. Providing employees with clear, actionable feedback not only clarifies what success looks like but also deepens their understanding and ability to meet these expectations in the future. Performance reviews must not be static, one-off events. Instead, they need to be dynamic, ongoing opportunities that enhance learning, and drive regular development and performance. By integrating regular performance reviews, organizations can create a culture where employees can be better engaged, motivated and thrive together in driving the organization's success.

To understand this further, let's take a closer look at **three key strategies** for effectively restoring regular performance reviews in an organization's culture.

1. Clarity of Expectations

This strategy helps ensure that employees understand their roles and responsibilities fully and have the resources and support they need to do their jobs effectively. This clarity not only helps employees with their performance but also helps them stay more focused and motivated.

An example of this is seen at MetLife, a U.S.-based global financial services company, with its "Leading the Future" program. Launched in 2021, the program is a comprehensive initiative aimed at supporting over 5,500 leaders across the organization. The program is designed to set clear expectations for all leadership roles while equipping managers and teams with the resources and tools they need to succeed. A vital feature of this initiative is the "Leader Expectations Tool". Introduced in 2022, this tool provides leaders with clear expectations of their roles, aligning them to the organization's strategic goals and helping them get ongoing feedback on their performance. The adoption of the tool has grown to over 4,300 managers in 2023 following its successful launch.

The effectiveness of MetLife's strategies in leadership development and employee engagement have also earned the organization significant recognition. In 2024, the organization was honored as one of the World's Best Workplaces by Fortune and certified as a Great Place To Work™. Their strategic focus on providing clear expectations and enhancing resources and support for all its leaders has been a core feature of their ongoing people strategy.

Through initiatives like the "Leading the Future" program, MetLife exemplifies how clarifying expectations and providing adequate resources and support to employees can make the performance review processes seamless, enhancing the impact of a results-based culture.

2. Mitigating Bias

In building a results-based culture, overcoming human bias is a constant challenge when it comes to performance reviews. Bias can easily creep into evaluations, distorting assessments and undermining trust. When employees feel their contributions are being judged unfairly or inconsistently, it demotivates them and weakens the credibility of the entire performance review process. Addressing this is essential to ensure fairness and consistency in the process and it requires a deliberate approach that emphasizes structure and objectivity in reviews.

The 360-degree review process is one way of addressing this. While the concept of 360 is not new, almost 90% of Fortune 500 companies now utilize some form of such feedback in their organization. The 360-degree review process, since being introduced to the business world in the 1950s by the former Esso Research and Engineering Group (now ExxonMobil), has since then evolved to include other aspects with it. One such aspect is Artificial Intelligence (AI). Organizations are seeing some advantages with using AI with the 360-degree review process. One advantage is that AI analytics can process feedback responses and generate key insights much faster and more effectively. In addition, it can identify patterns and trends, allowing the organization to pinpoint key strengths and areas for improvement for all employees much more effectively.

One organization that is effectively using AI-driven 360-degee feedback is IBM. All Employees at IBM are evaluated across five dimensions- business results, client success, innovation, personal responsibility and current skill sets. One of the ways the feedback process and dialogue is orchestrated is through an IBM app called ACE, which stands for Appreciation, Coaching, and Evaluation.

ACE allows an IBM employee to ask or give feedback to anyone, anytime in the organization. In addition, it also allows employees to learn the required skills for giving and asking for effective feedback. But, for any feedback to be effective, they need to not only be accurate but also fair. In this regard, ACE contains several algorithms, developed by a broader algorithmic fairness research community at IBM, to ensure accuracy of these algorithms from design to implementation. The team also makes sure that the coding pattern for ACE is constructed in a way to ensure fairness and help in effectively mitigating bias. In 2016, ACE was being used by over 90,000 IBM staffers (about 90% of the global workforce).

The integration of AI-driven 360-degree feedback systems, exemplified by IBM's ACE, represents a significant advancement in addressing the persistent challenge of human bias in performance reviews. By leveraging AI's analytical capabilities and implementing rigorous fairness algorithms, organizations can create more objective, consistent, and trustworthy evaluation processes. This approach not only enhances the accuracy of performance assessments but also fosters a culture of transparency, fairness, and continuous improvement. As more companies adopt these innovative solutions, we can expect to see a positive shift in employee engagement, motivation, and overall organizational performance, ultimately leading to more fair and equitable workplaces.

3. Task-Based Reviews

Another effective strategy for making performance reviews more impactful is through task-based reviews. This approach assesses performance for individuals based on specific projects or initiatives, rather than periodic or annual evaluations. Such a method provides a more immediate and relevant evaluation of an employee's effectiveness in their roles and functions. By evaluating the outcomes of specific projects, organizations can identify low and high performers much early, helping them adjust their actions and behaviors for future tasks.

The Taj Group of Hotels, part of Indian Hotels Company Limited (IHCL), reveals how task-based reviews can effectively create a results-based culture. Through its Taj People Philosophy (TPP) and Balanced Scorecard System (BSS), Taj integrates task-based reviews into its performance review process. The Balanced Scorecard System (BSS), introduced in 2003 under the TPP framework and being used even now, evaluates employee contributions across four key dimensions: financial outcomes, customer satisfaction, internal processes, and learning and growth. By focusing on these dimensions, Taj provides contextual and measurable feedback. For instance, during major events, employees are assessed based on tangible metrics like guest satisfaction scores and the efficiency of tasks. This ensures that performance reviews are tied directly to task-based objectives and contributions, enhancing accountability with timeliness of feedback. During the period 2006–2008, this played a key role in driving a 20% increase in guest satisfaction scores at some of its properties, and some properties reporting growth of up to 17% above market share.

Taj rewards employees for exceptional performance during specific tasks or customer interactions through the "Special Thanks and Recognition System" (STARS), offering recognition points for achieving high guest satisfaction scores, creating innovative solutions or displaying exemplary teamwork. The program has also evolved to include digital tracking of points via an internal app introduced in 2022, making it easier for employees to monitor their progress and receive timely recognition for their tasks.

The impact of Taj's task-based reviews, deeply intertwined with a sense of ownership, was profoundly evident during the November 26, 2008, Mumbai terror attacks. Amid the chaos, staff members demonstrated extraordinary bravery and selflessness, taking ownership of their tasks and prioritizing the safety and well-being of guests above everything else. Thomas Varghese, a senior waiter at the Wasabi restaurant, made sure all guests were evacuated before attempting to leave himself, a decision that tragically cost him his life. Similarly, Mallika Jagad, a banquet manager, acted with remarkable decisiveness, locking doors, switching off lights, and guiding her guests to safety, saving countless lives with her swift and courageous actions.

Both employees acted with conviction on their assigned tasks, and their composure and commitment under unimaginable pressure reflected a culture where employees not only completed their tasks but also made decisions that demonstrated the highest standards of service and humanity.

***

Over the course of this chapter, we've broken down what it takes to enhance and sustain a result-based culture one element at a time. By implementing some of the strategies and examples we've shared, you can begin laying a strong foundation for meaningful cultural restoration.

To tie it all together, let's revisit everything through a micro case study that shows how it all comes together in a thriving, restored organization.

How BHP Builds an effective Results-Based Culture

BHP Group, a leading mining organization based in Australia, demonstrates what a strong results-based culture can achieve by implementing effective accountability systems, clear performance metrics, and robust performance reviews. These elements work together to create an environment where employees are motivated, aligned, and empowered to contribute meaningfully to the organization's goals.

Accountability Systems

Accountability is a key aspect of BHP's results-based culture. The organization's "Our Code of Conduct" provides a strong foundation for ethical behavior and operational integrity. The Code outlines clear standards for compliance across all business units, ensuring that employees understand and uphold ethical practices in all their daily work. To reinforce these expectations, employees undergo mandatory training on the Code every year, embedding accountability into the organization's DNA.

BHP further ties accountability to performance outcomes through its incentive programs. When annual targets are not met, incentives are adjusted to reflect this. For instance, in certain fiscal years, performance shortfalls resulted in incentives being reduced by 20%. This approach underscores BHP's commitment to fairness and results and ensures that rewards are directly aligned with measurable achievements, reinforcing a culture where success is recognized, and accountability is expected.

To complement this, BHP conducts biannual Engagement and Perception Surveys to gather insights on employee satisfaction and alignment with the organization's mission. These surveys serve as a pulse check on how well employees connect with their work and the broader organizational goals. As of March 2024, 80% of employees reported feeling engaged, while 87% shared positive perceptions of their well-being. This data feeds into BHP's "Social Value Scorecard", a tool that reflects how individual and collective efforts contribute to the organization's broader priorities, including sustainability and employee growth.

Clear Performance Metrics

At the heart of BHP's results-based culture is its structured approach to measuring performance. Introduced in 2017, the BHP Operating System (BOS) serves as a key framework for aligning employee efforts with the organization's objectives. BOS focuses on continuous improvement and operational excellence, using data-driven strategies to track productivity, streamline operations, and ensure individual contributions aligned with its organizational goals.

For example, at the Newman iron ore operation in Western Australia, BOS led to a 40% increase in equipment lifespan – a significant improvement that reflects its focus on efficiency and measurable outcomes. Employees have a clear understanding of how their performance is measured using transparent metrics and integrated tools such as visual dashboards and real-time data tracking. Through implementing BOS and a culture of transparency, BHP has created a culture of performance where people feel empowered and accountable to drive results for the organization.

Regular Performance Reviews

At BHP, performance reviews play a key role in driving professional growth while fostering accountability across the organization. A standout initiative is the annual Gender Pay Equity Review, introduced in FY2018 as part of BHP's ongoing efforts to create an inclusive workplace. This review ensures that pay decisions are fair, transparent, and free from unconscious bias, addressing any systemic inequities that may exist. By prioritizing fairness, BHP strengthens trust among employees and reinforces its commitment to equal opportunities for all.

BHP has also taken meaningful steps to recognize and celebrate performance through its global recognition program, "Big Thanks | Muchas Gracias", launched in FY2020. This program acknowledges individual and team contributions that align with the organization's core priorities, including safety, innovation, and productivity. By FY2024, the program had recorded over 437,000 recognition moments across 16 countries. These acknowledgments, whether big or small, create a culture of appreciation at BHP, where employees feel motivated, valued, and connected to the organization's shared goals.

By deeply embedding accountability systems, clear performance metrics and regular performance review, BHP ensures that employees are motivated, focused, and aligned with its strategic priorities. This integration supports professional growth and creates a high-performance environment where individual contributions drive collective success for the organization long-term.

Reflective Assessment

Petal 6: Results-Based Culture

After reading the chapter, what is your current assessment of your organization's culture?

1. Accountability Systems

How well does your organization drive peer and cross-functional accountability?

....

....

....

What are some challenges you see in this regard and how do you plan to address them?

....

....

....

2. Clear Performance Metrics

How much clarity do your employees have on how their performance will be measured?

....

....

....

In what ways can you improve these further?

....

....

....

3. *Performance Reviews*

What strategies are you using in mitigating bias in your performance review process?

....

....

....

What are some areas that you still see need improvement?

....

....

....

Blooming to Full Potential

Reflecting on everything we've explored together; one thing becomes clear: Restoring cultures is powerful in transforming organizations. This journey has been about peeling away the layers of dysfunction or toxic cultures that many of us might have experienced and creating better workplaces that inspire us rather than frustrate or demoralize us. It has been about finding a way to restore workplaces into spaces where people and results can thrive together.

This work is deeply personal for us. Both of us have sat across from colleagues or friends at coffee shops, sharing stories of workplaces that left us feeling deflated or undervalued. Those conversations are all too familiar, filled with anecdotes of micromanagement, distrust, and burnout.

But what if those conversations could be different? What if the stories people shared about work were about growth, understanding, and well-being? That's why this work feels so important. Think about what it would be like to sit down with someone and hear them talk about how their workplace has embraced real listening, a place where well-being is supported, or how they've grown in ways they never thought possible. That's the movement we're working towards, where humanizing workplaces and achieving results can coexist in organizations, without any of them being compromised.

We have shared several moments from our conversations in these pages, but we would like to talk about one more because this captures our vision the best way. It came during a workshop we held at a non-profit organization in Singapore. As the session ended, Ken, one of the participants, came up to speak with us. He had recently joined the organization after leaving a tech company notorious for its toxic culture. Ken told us how, in his previous role, he had held onto hope that things would change. But over time, it became clear they wouldn't. *"It felt like no one cared about the people,"* he said. *"It was all about what you delivered and how fast you delivered it."*

When Ken joined his new company, he admitted he brought a lot of baggage with him- distrust, low expectations, and the sense that speaking up would only backfire. But something surprised him. His new workplace was trying to restore its culture with real action. Ken shared how he felt like his voice mattered for the first time in years. *"This place gave me space to unlearn the cynicism I brought with me,"* he told us. *"It's not perfect, but you can feel the difference. People care here."* Stories like Ken's inspire us to keep going because they show that cultural restoration is impactful and every effort towards it makes us more human.

Restoring cultures is about creating something better – it's about creating an environment where people feel valued, connected, and motivated to contribute. Toxic workplace cultures develop over time due to unresolved issues, unclear expectations, and a lack of empathy. Addressing these problems in a timely manner is essential for any organization. It requires a process that involves looking at deep-rooted issues and implementing meaningful changes that benefit all in the organization.

The FLOWER Framework™ provides a comprehensive way to approach this restoration. As you've seen, it focuses on six interconnected petals that work together to create a balanced and healthy workplace culture. These petals are designed to create a culture where everyone can thrive. Each petal plays a critical role in ensuring the restoration is effective and sustainable.

Fulfilling Culture: When employees feel their work has meaning and purpose, they are more engaged and motivated. This has a measurable impact on performance. People who feel fulfilled are more creative, productive, and focused. Prioritizing fulfillment can shift an organization from being disengaged to becoming high performing.

Listening culture: It ensures that when employees feel heard and understood, it builds trust and collaboration. When leaders and teams listen to understand, they create an environment where people feel safe to share ideas, raise concerns, and contribute fully. This level of openness helps prevent miscommunication and builds a foundation of trust that benefits everyone.

Ownership culture: This creates clarity and empowerment through transparency and openness. Employees feel motivated to do their best and feel empowered to actively look to solve problems. As a result, they work together collaboratively, shifting their focus away from assigning blame to taking responsibility for their actions.

Well-being culture: A culture that prioritizes well-being makes a clear commitment to its employees by offering autonomy at work, flexible work arrangements, wellness resources and supportive leadership. These efforts create an environment where employees feel cared for, improving their energy and focus, and in turn improving the overall health and performance of the organization.

Enterprising Culture: It encourages employees to approach challenges with creativity and flexibility, encouraging them to explore new ideas and take calculated risks. This kind of culture is crucial in today's fast-paced world, where organizations need to stay agile to respond to complex challenges. Employees in an enterprising culture know their contributions matter, and this confidence drives innovation by bringing their best ideas forward.

Results-based culture: This helps employees understand how their daily efforts contribute to bigger organizational goals, making their work feel more meaningful. By focusing on measurable outcomes rather than just completing tasks, teams eliminate ambiguity, build accountability and help everyone achieve transformational results.

The six petals of the framework come together cohesively to cultivate a workplace where everyone feels positively engaged. The framework works because it is adaptable. Every organization has its own challenges and priorities, and the framework allows flexibility in how each element is addressed. By focusing on what matters most while keeping all the pieces connected, organizations can create meaningful, long-lasting change. This adaptability ensures that restoration goes deep enough to make a difference but is practical enough to succeed in real-world settings.

We've come across some fascinating statistics within these pages that highlight the impact of restoring and strengthening workplace cultures. Research consistently highlights the undeniable and measurable advantages of cultivating a strong, restored organizational culture. A study from the Great Place To Work™ in 2022 reveals the profound impact of culture on employee satisfaction and organizational performance. In its analysis of CDK Global India, a leading provider of retail technology and software, the results revealed that CDK's healthy workplace culture led to an increase in employee satisfaction scores from 74% in 2020 to 90% in 2022.

Similarly, a 2020 CEO survey conducted by Heidrick & Struggles underscores the financial benefits of prioritizing culture. Organizations referred to as "culture accelerators" in the study made a deliberate effort to align their core values with their business strategies. This alignment resulted in notable improvements in financial performance, demonstrating the power of culture as a driver of success. Specifically, these organizations reported a three-year compound annual growth rate (CAGR) of 9.1%, more than double the 4.4% CAGR of other organizations surveyed.

With Artificial Intelligence (AI) evolving so quickly and technology constantly changing, it's more important more than ever to focus on culture. While AI holds immense promises for enhancing productivity, streamlining operations, and driving innovation, it also brings challenges, including job insecurity, ethical dilemmas, and the potential to weaken interpersonal connections.

McKinsey's report, The State of Organizations 2023, published in April 2023, highlights that organizations effectively leveraging AI are nearly three times more likely to cultivate a culture of continuous learning and collaboration. However, achieving this requires intentional efforts to maintain a focus on being human-centered. Companies must integrate AI in ways that align with their core values, emphasizing empathy, adaptability, and employee well-being. For this, culture needs to be at the forefront of any organization.

The urgency of this is shown by the World Economic Forum's prediction of a 23% job churn by 2027 due to AI-driven roles. This makes it imperative for organizations to prioritize upskilling and reskilling while looking at various subcultures explored in the FLOWER Framework™. By embracing the framework, organizations can tackle this technological evolution thoughtfully, ensuring they don't lose sight of their most important asset – their people.

When we reflect on everything discussed so far, one key aspect stands out as critical and essential to the restoration of an organization's culture: the active and consistent involvement of leadership. This is why, when we first started exploring the idea of cultural restoration, we began with the concept of restored leadership. Over time, as we delved deeper, we realized that while leadership alone cannot achieve the full restoration that's needed in organizations, it was undoubtedly the cornerstone for any meaningful and sustainable cultural change.

Leaders set the tone for what an organization stands for. Their actions, words, and decisions communicate to employees what is important, and when leaders actively demonstrate and live the organizational values, they become culture carriers, modeling behaviors that ripple across teams and departments. For example, when leaders prioritize well-being through their own actions, they send a powerful message to the rest of the organization. Consider a senior executive visibly supporting flexible work arrangements or participating in a mental health awareness program. Such actions resonate deeply with employees, build trust in them and encourage them to do the same through their own actions.

Leadership involvement also becomes critical during times of change. Whether it's a merger, a restructuring, or adaptation to a new market, employees look to leaders for guidance and support. Leaders who are engaged and transparent during these critical moments help stabilize the organization, keeping employees reassured and aligned with the strategic direction of the organization.

At the heart of such leadership lies the philosophy of empathy. At its core, this leadership trait goes beyond the usual metrics of organizations and focuses on the people who drive the organization forward. This approach has a profound impact on employee engagement and loyalty. When employees sense genuine care from leadership, their connection to the organization deepens. They are more likely to give their best, knowing their efforts are recognized and their well-being matters. Empathetic leadership also acts as a magnet for talent, drawing individuals who seek a workplace where they are respected and cared for.

Throughout our discussions, we've looked at what happens when organizations lead with empathy, care, and respect. Leaders such as the ones mentioned throughout the book- late Major Surajan, Dr. Peggy Crowe, Ho Kwon Peng, Richard Branson, and Dr. Roland Smith- all demonstrate these traits and show us the powerful and positive impact that leadership can have on restored cultures.

Restoration demands courage and commitment and holds the promise of real transformation. It is about building something stronger, creating something more human, with an eye on business outcomes. Michael Bush in his book, "A Great Place to Work For All," highlights the story of Heather Brunner, CEO of WP Engine, a US website creation company. When Heather joined as CEO in 2013, she made a risky decision to drop the requirement of a four-year college degree for any job application. It was a courageous decision since 69% of US employers at that time made college degrees mandatory for entry-level jobs. But Heather envisioned a future where all people, no matter what their background or education, can have a chance to be part of the tech industry. Her vision paid off, and WP Engine's business grew tenfold within a span of 4 years since she joined. Heather went against the norm of the industry and her peers in leading with inclusion and showed courage to create a workplace where both people and results could thrive.

In this book, we have given examples of numerous organizations and leaders who took courageous steps to stand apart from others in their industry to make a positive difference. Courage takes time and effort. No leader wakes up in the morning and says, "*I think I am going to fundamentally change the organization today.*" It requires thoughtful planning and strategy.

Restoration is a journey, and through this book, we invite you to step into this journey and have restorative conversations with the people around you, with intent and an open mind. Change begins with a single step, and so we encourage leaders and organizations to take the first courageous step and start with a clear assessment of where their current culture is in relation to the six petals mentioned in this book and reflect on what bold steps need to be taken to restore their workplace culture fully.

Through this deliberate and thoughtful approach, organizations can move away from toxicity and create workplaces where meaningful connections flourish and an engaged workforce drives results that matter.

We would like to quote the words of another leader mentioned earlier in the book, Piyush Gupta of DBS, who said, *"I was really focused on culture by design. When you get the culture right, you get an organization where a thousand flowers can bloom."* His words brilliantly capture how organizations can bloom to their fullest potential when they display courage in restoring their cultures through the FLOWER Framework™.

Season after season, the flowers can be in full bloom. A thousand bright, bold, and beautiful blossoms burst forth, symbolizing 'The Restored Organization'.

Author's Note

In this book, we've explored how organizations can restore their cultures and become places where people feel respected, valued, and fulfilled. But we know that for someone stuck in a toxic workplace right now, this might feel distant or even impossible. The pain of working in a toxic environment is deeply personal and immediate. If you're reading this and find yourself in that place right now, we want to pause and speak directly to you.

We've been there. We know what it's like to feel drained, overlooked, or even diminished by a workplace or leader that doesn't see your value. It's exhausting, and it can leave you doubting yourself. That's why we want to share this small note with you- because we believe in your strength, and we want you to know you're not alone.

What You Can Do Right Now

- ➤ **Take Care of Yourself First:** Your health matters more than the job you have. Find ways to protect your mental and emotional well-being. This might mean stepping away from work for a moment, whether it's taking a short break or just pausing to breathe.
- ➤ **Talk to Someone You Trust:** Whether it's a friend, a family member, or a mentor, sharing what you're going through can make a big difference. It helps to have someone remind you of your worth when the environment around you doesn't.
- ➤ **Look to the Future:** Think about what you need to feel happy and supported at work. Start exploring other options, even if it's just small steps. It can give you a sense of hope and direction.

What to Avoid

- ➤ **Don't Carry the Blame:** This isn't your fault. Toxicity in the workplace reflects on the organization, not on you. Please don't let their failures make you question your worth.
- ➤ **Don't Burn Yourself Out:** It's easy to keep pushing yourself to prove something, but you don't need to. Your worth isn't tied to how much you endure.
- ➤ **Don't Lose Sight of Who You Are:** A toxic environment can make you feel small, but it doesn't define you. Hold on to your strengths, talents, and the things that make you unique.

If you ever feel the need to share your story or need a bit of guidance, please reach out to us at *info@therestoredorganization.com*. You are not alone on this journey, and you don't have to figure it all out by yourself. We're here to remind you that no matter how heavy things feel right now, this isn't the end of your story. Better workplaces, better days, and better possibilities are ahead. Take care of yourself. You deserve it.

***

We can support your organization in three ways:
1. Keynote speaker at conferences, events or leadership offsites.
2. Facilitate a Masterclass or workshop for your leaders and teams.
3. One-on-one personalized coaching or team coaching.

For more information visit *www.therestoredorganization.com*

Appendix 1

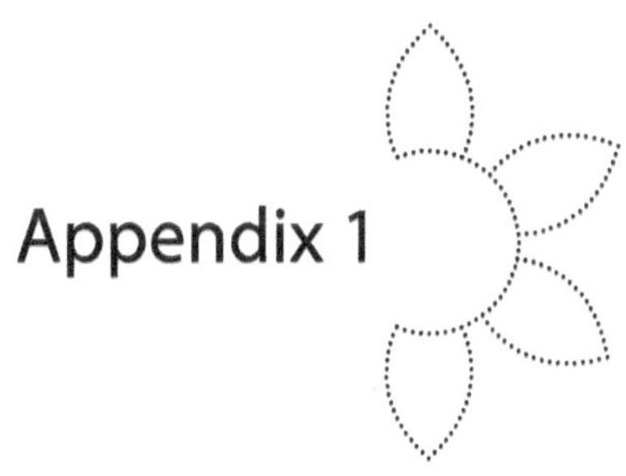

Content Navigator

Petal 1: Fulfilling Culture

Elements	Strategy	Examples	Page
Purpose	1. Role Modeling	Major Surajan, Singapore	65
	2. Authentic Storytelling	Atlassian, Australia	66
	3. Purpose-Driven Initiatives	Unilever, UK	67
Recognition	1. Tie Recognition to Values	Wipro, India	69
	2. Peer Recognition	Southwest Airlines, USA	70
	3. Personalization	Disney, USA	71
Career Development	1. Core Focus	Hilton, USA	73
	2. Mentorship	Caterpillar, USA	74
	3. Internal Mobility	Schneider Electric, France	75

Micro Case Study: *Patagonia, USA.*

Petal 2: Listening Culture

Elements	Strategy	Examples	Page
Active Listening	1. Reflective Conversations	Dr. Peggy Crowe, USA	87
	2. Peer-to-Peer Listening	Reuters, UK	89
	3. Leadership Involvement	Nissan Group, USA	90
Open Feedback Channels	1. Feedback from All Levels	Micron Technology, Singapore	92
	2. Ongoing Feedback	American Express, USA	93
	3. Timely Action	Medtronic, USA	93
Commitment to Inclusion	1. Transparency in Decision-Making	IHG Hotels & Resorts, UK	95
	2. Elevating Underrepresented Voices	Intel, USA	96
	3. Regular Assessments	Zuellig Pharma, Philippines	97

Micro Case Study: *Netflix, United States*

Petal 3: Ownership Culture

Elements	Strategy	Examples	Page
Empower-ment	1. Delegate Authority	Bayer, Germany	109
	2. Meaningful Contributions	Extra•Ordinary People, Singapore	110
	3. Continuous Engagement	Tata Motors, India	111
Shared Goals	1. Co-Creation	United Overseas Bank, Singapore	113
	2. Regular Communication	H&M, Sweden	114
	3. Effective Collaboration	LEGO, Denmark	115
Transparent Communica-tion	1. Authentic Leadership	Ho Kwon Ping, Singapore	118
	2. Ongoing Conversations	AbbVie, USA	119
	3. Leveraging Technology	Chalhoub Group, UAE	120

Micro Case Study: *Yara International, Norway*

Petal 4: Well-being Culture

Elements	Strategy	Examples	Page
Holistic Programs	1. Organizational Alignment	Google, USA	131
	2. Personalization	Swiggy, India	132
	3. Continued Evaluation	Danone, France	133
Work-Life Integration	1. Flexibility	HSBC, UK	136
	2. Leadership Behavior	Richard Branson, UK	136
	3. Encouraging Time Off	Canva, Australia	137
Supportive Environment	1. Wellness Ambassadors	Spotify, Sweden	139
	2. Peer Support Networks	Kaiser Permanente, USA	140
	3. Digital Tools	Microsoft, USA	142

Micro Case Study: *Johnson & Johnson, USA*

Petal 5: Enterprising Culture

Elements	Strategy	Examples	Page
Innovation Incentives	1. Mixed Incentives Models	Mars Inc., USA	153
	2. External Partnerships	Singapore Airlines, Singapore	154
	3. Gamification	Cisco Systems Inc., USA	155
Collaborative Spaces	1. Creating Safe Spaces	Dr. Roland Smith, Singapore	157
	2. Adaptability	Mayo Clinic, USA	159
	3. Leadership Vision	Pixar, USA	160
Continuous Learning	1. Knowledge-Sharing Platform	Hindustan Unilever Limited, India	162
	2. Cross-Functional Learning	Philip Morris International, USA	163
	3. Leveraging Artificial Intelligence (AI)	DBS Bank, Singapore	164

Micro Case Study: *DHL Express, Germany*

Petal 6: Results-Based Culture

Elements	Strategy	Examples	Page
Accountability Systems	1. Peer Accountability	W.L. Gore & Associates, USA	176
	2. Cross-Functional Accountability	Azbil Corporation, Japan	177
	3. Role-Specific Accountability	Hyundai Motors, India	178
Clear Performance Metrics	1. Goal-Setting Frameworks	Domino's Pizza, USA	180
	2. Data Governance	Celcom, Malaysia	181
	3. Leading and Lagging Indicators	Mizuho Bank, Japan	183
Regular Performance Reviews	1. Clarity of Expectations	MetLife, USA	185
	2. Mitigating Bias	IBM, USA	186
	3. Task-Based Reviews	Taj Group of Hotels, India	187

Micro Case Study: *BHP Group, Australia*

Appendix 2

References

- Antonovsky, A. (1979). Health, stress and coping. San Francisco: Jossey-Bass Publishers.
- Petery, G., Parker, S., & Zoszak, L. (2020). The importance of psychological contracts for safe work during pandemics. Journal of Applied Psychology. Retrieved from Curtin University Repository.
- Gutelius, B., & Pinto, S. (2023). *Pain Points: Data on Work Intensity, Monitoring, and Health at Amazon Warehouses*. Center for Urban Economic Development, University of Illinois, Chicago.
- Kotaku (2019, December 6). Razer CEO Accused of Threatening and Publicly Shaming Employees. Retrieved from *https://kotaku.com*
- Mothership.sg (2019, December 6). Razer CEO Tan Min-Liang Called a 'Dictator' by Ex-Employees. Retrieved from *https://mothership.sg*
- Indian Express. (2024, September 20). After Pune CA dies, mother alleges 'work pressure'; EY India denies. Retrieved from *https://indianexpress.com*
- Lyra Health (2024). Toxic Work Environment: How to Spot the Signs and Fix It. Retrieved from *https://www.lyrahealth.com*
- Gordon, E. (2014, April 20). The brain's organizing principle. Myelin Leadership. Retrieved from *https://myelinleadership.com/2014/04/20/the-brains-organizing-principle/*
- Weise, K., & Kantor, J. (2021, June 15). Inside Amazon's employment machine. The New York Times. Retrieved from *https://www.nytimes.com*

➤ Rijksmuseum (2019). Operation Night Watch. Retrieved from the Rijksmuseum website: *https://www.rijksmuseum.nl/en/whats-on/exhibitions/operation-night-watch*

➤ World Wide Fund for Nature Singapore (WWF-Singapore). (n.d.). Nature & biodiversity: Forest landscape restoration. Retrieved from WWF-Singapore website: *https://www.wwf.sg/nature-biodiversity/*

➤ Friends of the High Line (2024). Design and transformation of the High Line. Retrieved from The High Line website: *https://www.thehighline.org/design/*

➤ Zak, P. J. (2017). Trust Factor: The Science of Creating High-Performance Companies. American Management Association.

➤ Zak, P. J., Barraza, J., & Alexander, V. (2020). The neuroscience of organisational trust and business performance. Frontiers in Psychology. *https://doi.org/10.3389/fpsyg.2020.579459*

➤ Zaki, J. (2019). The War for Kindness: Building Empathy in a Fractured World. Crown Publishing Group.

➤ Rizzolatti, G., & Sinigaglia, C. (2008). Mirrors in the brain: How our minds share actions and emotions. Oxford University Press.

➤ Nadella, S., & Shaw, G. (2017). Hit Refresh: The Quest to Rediscover Microsoft's Soul and Imagine a Better Future for Everyone. Harper Business.

➤ People and Future of Work 2023 (Singtel). Retrieved from *https://www.singtel.com/about-us/sustainability/sustainability-at-singtel/people*

➤ Korn Ferry (2024). The importance of inclusion in the workplace. Retrieved from the Korn Ferry website: *https://www.kornferry.com*

➤ Cedars-Sinai (2024). The science of kindness. Retrieved from Cedars-Sinai website: *https://www.cedars-sinai.org*

➤ DBS Bank (2022). DBS named to Bloomberg Gender-Equality Index for the fifth consecutive year. Retrieved from the DBS website: *https://www.dbs.com/newsroom/DBS_named_to_Bloomberg_Gender_Equality_Index_for_fifth_consecutive_year_sg5*

➤ McKinsey & Company (2023). Leading from the front: How DBS embraces change and empowers employees. Retrieved from the

McKinsey website: *https://www.mckinsey.com/capabilities/people-and-organizational-performance/our-insights/leading-from-the-front-how-dbs-embraces-change-and-empowers-employees*

➤ Kent Business School. (2017). Uber CEO quit due to 'toxic' culture and lack of profits. Retrieved from Kent Business School website: *https://blogs.kent.ac.uk/kbs-news-events/2017/07/expert-comment-uber-ceo-quit-due-to-toxic-culture-and-lack-of-profits/*

➤ Business Insider (2016). IBM changes its employee reviews. Retrieved from the Business Insider website: *https://www.businessinsider.com/ibm-changes-its-employee-reviews-2016-2*

➤ Evernote (2022). Work from (almost) anywhere: How Evernote has embraced the future of remote work. Retrieved from the Evernote website: *https://evernote.com/blog/evernote-future-remote-work*

➤ Mønster, D., Håkonsson, D. D., Eskildsen, J. K., & Wallot, S. (2016). Physiological evidence of interpersonal dynamics in a cooperative production task. Physiology & Behavior, 156, 24–34. *https://doi.org/10.1016/j.physbeh.2016.01.004*

➤ Forbes (2022). How chronic work stress damages your brain- and 10 things you can do. Retrieved from *https://www.forbes.com*

➤ Maslow, A. H. (1954). Motivation and Personality. Harper.

➤ Spreng, R. N., Sepulcre, J., Turner, G. R., Stevens, W. D., & Schacter, D. L. (2013). Intrinsic architecture underlying the relations among the default, dorsal attention, and frontoparietal control networks in the human brain. Journal of Cognitive Neuroscience, 25(1), 74–86. *https://doi.org/10.1162/jocn_a_00281*

➤ Atlassian (2024). Humans of Atlassian. Retrieved from the Atlassian website: *https://www.atlassian.com/company/careers/resources/culture/humans-of-atlassian*

➤ Atlassian (2024). Company culture, company values: Why do they matter? Retrieved from the Atlassian website: *https://www.atlassian.com/blog/distributed-work/company-culture-company-values*

➤ Harvard Business Review. (2022, March). Use purpose to transform your workplace. Retrieved from *https://hbr.org/2022/03/use-purpose-to-transform-your-workplace*

➤ London School of Economics & Unilever. (2023). The link between purpose and motivation. Retrieved from the Unilever website: *https://www.unilever.com/sustainability/future-of-work/providing-skills-for-life/*

➤ Wise, R. A. (2004). Dopamine, learning and motivation. Nature Reviews Neuroscience, 5(6), 483–494. *https://doi.org/10.1038/nrn1406*

➤ The Print. (2024). Tech giant achieves cultural transformation through an innovative recognition & rewards programme. Retrieved from *https://theprint.in/ani-press-releases/tech-giant-achieves-cultural-transformation-through-innovative-recognition-rewards-programme/2160499/*

➤ SHRM (n.d.). Wipro's innovative approach: A recognition & rewards program success. Retrieved from *https://www.shrm.org/in/topics-tools/news/wipros-innovative-approach-a-recognition-rewards-program-success*

➤ O.C. Tanner (2023). Southwest Airlines: Recognising the employee journey with heart. Retrieved from *https://www.octanner.com/client-stories/southwest-airlines*

➤ Disney Impact (2023). RecognizeNow! is a worldwide digital platform for our employees that enables them to send notes of appreciation, recognition, and gratitude quickly and easily. Retrieved from *https://thewaltdisneycompany.eu/app/uploads/2024/04/TWDC-EMEA-CSR-Report_2023.pdf*

➤ Disney Life at Disney (2024). Meet a custodial cast member making magic at Disney California Adventure. Retrieved from *https://sites.disney.com/lifeatdisney/career-opportunities/2024/01/03/custodial-cast-member-disney-california-adventure/*

➤ Disney Life at Disney (2023). Celebrating the Walt Disney Legacy Award APAC recipients. Retrieved from *https://sites.disney.com/lifeatdisney/employee-stories/2023/02/01/celebrating-the-walt-disney-legacy-award-apac-recipients/*

➤ Deci, E. L., & Ryan, R. M. (1985). Intrinsic motivation and self-determination in human behavior. Springer Science & Business Media.

➤ International Youth Foundation (2023). Hilton increases employee retention with Passport to Success. Retrieved from *https://www.*

➢ *passporttosuccess.org/case-studies/hilton-increases-employee-retention-passport-success*

➢ Hilton (2020). Team member engagement: Learning and development. Retrieved from *https://cr.hilton.com/wp-content/uploads/2020/04/Hilton-Team-Member-Engagement.pdf*

➢ Caterpillar (2023). Employee resource groups: Mentorship and professional development. Retrieved from *https://www.caterpillar.com/en/careers/why-caterpillar/employee-resource-groups.html*

➢ Caterpillar (2023). Developing our people: Leadership and technical development programmes. Retrieved from *https://www.caterpillar.com/en/company/sustainability/sustainability-report/focus-areas/power-of-everyone/developing-people.html*

➢ Gloat (2023). How Schneider Electric increased employee retention. Retrieved from *https://gloat.com/resources/customer-stories-2/how-schneider-electric-increased-employee-retention/*

➢ Patagonia (2023). Our Core Values. Retrieved from *https://www.patagonia.com/our-footprint/corporate-social-responsibility-history.html*

➢ Chouinard, Y. (2016). Let My People Go Surfing: The Education of a Reluctant Businessman (Revised ed.). Penguin Books.

➢ HRD Connect (2024). Patagonia: Driving purpose with the Earth University. Retrieved from *https://www.hrdconnect.com/casestudy/casestudy-earth-university-aligning-purpose-passion-and-profits-at-patagonia/*

➢ Rogers, C. R., & Farson, R. E. (1957). Active Listening. Reprinted in 1987 in D. Kolb, I. Rubin, & J. McIntyre (Eds.), Organizational Psychology: A Book of Readings (3rd ed.). Mockingbird Press.

➢ Bodie, G. D., Vickery, A. J., Cannava, K., & Jones, S. M. (2015). Perceiving active listening: The role of trait mindfulness and empathic concern. Communication Research Reports, 32(3), 272-280.

➢ Kamitani, K., & Hiraiwa-Hasegawa, M. (2014). Perceiving active listening activates the reward system and emotional processing regions: An fMRI study. Frontiers in Neuroscience. *https://doi.org/10.3389/fnins.2014.00257*

➤ International Press Institute. (2022). Structured peer support network. OnTheLine. Retrieved from *https://newsrooms-ontheline.ipi.media/measures/structured-peer-support-network/*

➤ NASA Academy of Program/Project & Engineering Leadership (APPEL). (2015). After-action review: Best practices and lessons learned. Retrieved from *https://appel.nasa.gov/wp-content/uploads/2015/11/After-Action-Review_V3.pdf*

➤ Great Place To Work™ (2023). How listening programs helped Nissan boost employee survey results. Retrieved from *https://www.greatplacetowork.com/resources/case-studies/employee-listening-nissan-boost-survey*

➤ Edmondson, A. C. (1999). Psychological safety and learning behaviour in work teams. Administrative Science Quarterly, 44(2), 350-383. *https://doi.org/10.2307/2666999*

➤ Micron Technology (2020). Engagement & retention: Sustainability report. Retrieved from *https://www.micron.com/content/dam/micron/global/public/documents/about/sustainability/sustainability-report-2020.pdf*

➤ American Express. (2024). American Express Investor Day 2024. Retrieved from *https://s26.q4cdn.com/747928648/files/doc_downloads/2024/04/American-Express-Investor-Day-2024.pdf*

➤ Great Place To Work™ (2024). American Express - Great Place To Work™. Retrieved from *https://www.greatplacetowork.com/certified-company/1000311*

➤ Medtronic (2020). The People Behind Our Mission: 2020 Global Inclusion, Diversity, and Equity Report. Retrieved from *https://news.medtronic.com/2020-inclusion-diversity-and-equity-report*

➤ Medtronic (2023). Zero barriers: Driving impact - Global Inclusion, Diversity & Equity 2023 Annual Report. Retrieved from *https://www.medtronic.com/en-us/our-impact/ide-report.html*

➤ InterContinental Hotels Group (IHG). (2022). Governance Report: Annual Report and Form 20-F 2022. Retrieved from *https://www.ihgplc.com/~/media/Files/I/Ihg-Plc/investors/corporate-governance/governance.pdf*

➤ Intel Corporation (2023). 2023-24 Corporate Responsibility Report. Retrieved from *https://csrreportbuilder.intel.com/pdfbuilder/pdfs/CSR-2023-24-Full-Report.pdf*

➤ Business for Social Responsibility (BSR) (2021). Conducting a DEI assessment in Asia Pacific: Case study with Zuellig Pharma. Retrieved from *https://www.bsr.org/en/case-studies/conducting-a-dei-assessment-in-asia-pacific-apac*

➤ Zuellig Pharma (2021). Sustainability framework: Nurturing talent and fostering diversity, equity, and inclusion. Retrieved from *https://www.zuelligpharma.com/about-us/sustainability/sustainability-framework*

➤ Hastings, R. (2023). Netflix Culture Memo. Netflix. Retrieved from *https://www.netflix.com/culture*

➤ Koller, D., & Harter, J. (2023). The impact of active listening on employee engagement at Netflix. Journal of Organizational Behavior, 44(1), 72-88. *https://doi.org/10.1002/job.2635*

➤ Stanford Graduate School of Business. (2023). The transparency advantage: How Netflix's inclusive decision-making fosters a culture of listening. Stanford Business Review. Retrieved from *https://www.gsb.stanford.edu*

➤ USC Annenberg Inclusion Initiative (2023). Representation in entertainment: An analysis of diversity in Netflix content and workforce. University of Southern California. Retrieved from *https://annenberg.usc.edu*

➤ Hitchcock, D. E., & Willard, M. L. (1995). Why teams can fail and what to do about it: Essential tools for anyone implementing self-directed work teams. McGraw-Hill.

➤ Corporate Rebels (2024). How Bayer transitions to self-management with 100,000 employees. Retrieved from *https://www.corporate-rebels.com/blog/how-bayer-transitions-to-self-management-with-100-000-employees*

➤ Bayer. (2024). Bayer aims to sustainably improve performance with new organization. Retrieved from *https://www.bayer.com/media/en-us/bayer-aims-to-sustainably-improve-performance-with-new-organization/*

➤ Reimaginaire (2024). Reinventing big pharma: Bayer's shift towards dynamic shared ownership. Retrieved from *https://reimaginaire.*

medium.com/reinventing-big-pharma-bayers-shift-towards-dynamic-shared-ownership-341c30be73b5#:~:text=Early%20results%20of%20the%20DSO,expanded%20footprint%20in%20the%20U.S.

➤ Tata Motors (2024). Catalysing culture: Unleashing the power within organisations. Retrieved from *https://www.tatamotors.com/blog/catalysing-culture-unleashing-the-power-within-organisations/*

➤ People Matters (2024). AMP culture: Tata Motors' strategy to navigate cultural transformation. Retrieved from *https://www.peoplematters.in/amp-culture-tata-motors-strategy-to-navigate-cultural-transformation-41468*

➤ UOB Group (2022). UOB expands Gig+U programme to women with caregiving duties. Retrieved from *https://www.uobgroup.com/uobgroup/newsroom/2022/uob-expands-gigu-programme-to-women.page?path=data%2Fuobgroup%2F2022%2F251&cr=segment*

➤ The Straits Times. (n.d.). UOB: No meetings beyond office hours, project-based flexi-work to retain talent. Retrieved from *https://www.straitstimes.com/singapore/jobs/uob-no-meetings-beyond-office-hours-project-based-flexi-work-retain-talent*

➤ Case Study: H&M; *https://www.oneteam.io/en/case-studies/hm*

➤ EFMD Global (2023). The LEGO Group & IMD: Leadership Playground. Retrieved from *https://www.efmdglobal.org/wp-content/uploads/LEGO-IMD-EiP2023-FullCase.pdf*

➤ The CFO. (2024). Retrieved from *https://the-cfo.io/2024/10/25/105484/*

➤ MIT Sloan Management Review (2024). How the LEGO Group built culture change from the ground up. Retrieved from *https://sloanreview.mit.edu/article/how-the-lego-group-built-culture-change-from-the-ground-up/*

➤ Summerfield, C., & Egner, T. (2009). Expectation (and attention) in visual cognition. Trends in Cognitive Sciences, 13(9), 403–409. *https://doi.org/10.1016/j.tics.2009.06.003*

➤ Kok, P., Jehee, J. F., & de Lange, F. P. (2012). Less is more: Expectation sharpens representations in the primary visual cortex. Neuron, 75(2), 265–270. *https://doi.org/10.1016/j.neuron.2012.04.034*

➤ Singapore Management University. (2024). Ho Kwon Ping tells why he is a good leader, not a great one. Retrieved from *https://news.smu.edu.sg/news/2024/05/22/ho-kwon-ping-tells-why-he-good-leader-not-great-one*

➤ The Straits Times. (2024). 'I could never be a great leader because I'm not selfless enough': Ho Kwon Ping. Retrieved from *https://www.straitstimes.com/singapore/i-could-never-be-a-great-leader-because-i-m-not-selfless-enough-ho-kwon-ping*

➤ BBC News (2010). Retrieved from *https://www.bbc.com/news/11910973*

➤ Cooler Insights. (2024). Banyan Tree: Building a global luxury brand. Retrieved from *https://coolerinsights.com/2024/08/banyan-tree-building-a-global-luxury-brand/*

➤ AbbVie (2018). How our uniquely AbbVie culture drives employee engagement. Retrieved from *https://www.linkedin.com/pulse/how-our-uniquely-abbvie-culture-drives-employee-tim-richmond*

➤ VU Research Portal. (2020). Performance management at AbbVie. Retrieved from *https://research.vu.nl/ws/portalfiles/portal/233616894/Performance_Management_at_AbbVie.pdf*

➤ Beekeeper (2024). Chalhoub Group case study. Retrieved from *https://www.beekeeper.io/resources/success-stories/chalhoub/*

➤ Chalhoub Group (2023). Sustainability Report 2023. Retrieved from *https://api.chalhoubgroup.com/content/uploads/sustainability/SUSTAINABILITY-REPORT-23-0705—REDUCED.pdf*

➤ Yara International (2023). Employee share purchase programme. Retrieved from *https://www.yara.com/corporate-releases/yara-employee-share-purchase-program2/*

➤ Yara International (2023). Diversity, equity, and inclusion programmes. Retrieved from *https://www.yara.com/careers/life-at-yara/diversity-equity-inclusion/*

➤ Yara International. (2023). Integrated Report 2023. Retrieved from *https://www.yara.com/investor-relations/latest-annual-report/*

➤ Yara International. (2024). Third-quarter report 2024. Retrieved from *https://www.yara.com/siteassets/investors/057-reports-and-presentations/quarterly-reports/2024/3q-2024/yara-3q-2024-report.pdf*

➤ Sapolsky, R. M. (2004). Why stress is bad for your brain. Science, 308(5722), 648-649. *https://doi.org/10.1126/science.1112050*

➤ McEwen, B. S., & Morrison, J. H. (2013). The brain on stress: Vulnerability and plasticity of the prefrontal cortex over the life course. Neuron, 79(1), 16-29. *https://doi.org/10.1016/j.neuron.2013.06.028*

➤ Google (2021). COVID-19 & Well-being - Google Diversity Equity & Inclusion. Retrieved from *https://about.google/belonging/diversity-annual-report/2021/covid-19-wellbeing/*

➤ Forbes (2018). How Google's strategy for happy employees boosts its bottom line. Retrieved from *https://www.forbes.com/sites/pavelkrapivin/2018/09/17/how-googles-strategy-for-happy-employees-boosts-its-bottom-line/*

➤ Swiggy (2020). Swiggy launches wellness program 'Built Around You'. Retrieved from *https://www.swiggy.com/corporate/wp-content/uploads/2024/10/Annual-report-2020-2021.pdf*

➤ Fortune India (2023). Swiggy's mantra: Wellness & wealth. Retrieved from *https://www.fortuneindia.com/long-reads/swiggys-mantra-wellness-wealth/116284*

➤ Danone. (2023). Danone Employees' Health and Well-being. Retrieved from *https://www.danone.com/content/dam/corp/global/danonecom/about-us-impact/policies-and-commitments/en/2024/danone-employees-health-and-wellbeing.pdf*

➤ Danone (2023). Integrated Annual Report 2023. Retrieved from *https://www.danone.com/content/dam/corp/global/danonecom/investors/en-all-publications/2023/integratedreports/integratedannualreport2023.pdf*

➤ McEwen, B. S., & Morrison, J. H. (2013). The brain on stress: Vulnerability and plasticity of the prefrontal cortex over the life course. Neuron, 79(1), 16–29. *https://doi.org/10.1016/j.neuron.2013.06.028*

➤ HSBC Holdings plc. (2023). Interim Report 2023. Retrieved from *https://www.hsbc.com/-/files/hsbc/investors/hsbc-results/2023/interim/pdfs/hsbc-holdings-plc/230801-interim-report-2023.pdf*

➤ The Economic Times. (2010, June 28). HSBC offers flexible working hours to staff. Retrieved from *https://economictimes.indiatimes.com/jobs/hsbc-offers-flexible-working-hours-to-staff/articleshow/6099814.cms*

- People Matters Global. (2023). Inside HSBC's permanent hybrid work model. Retrieved from *https://www.peoplemattersglobal.com/news/employee-engagement/inside-hsbcs-permanent-hybrid-work-model-30763*

- Forbes (2023) CEOs Quit in Record Numbers in 2023. Retrieved from *https://www.forbes.com/sites/julianhayesii/2024/02/26/the-great-ceo-resignation-of-2023-3-keys-to-improving-ceo-well-being/*

- Richard Branson on Healthy Leadership and Organizational Well-Being. Retrieved from *https://www.futureofbusinessandtech.com/employee-well-being/richard-branson-on-healthy-leadership-and-organisational-well-being/*

- Canva (2024). Benefits and ways of working. Retrieved from *https://www.lifeatcanva.com/en/our-culture/benefits-ways-of-working/*

- Jake Law (2024). 'Right to Disconnect': New law enhances work-life balance. Retrieved from *https://jakelaw.com.au/right-to-disconnect/*

- Zak, P. J., Stanton, A. A., & Ahmadi, S. (2007). Oxytocin increases generosity in humans. PLoS ONE, 2(11), e1128. *https://doi.org/10.1371/journal.pone.0001128*

- Beaty, R. E., Benedek, M., Kaufman, S. B., & Silvia, P. J. (2015). Default and executive network coupling support creative idea production. Scientific Reports, 5, 10964. *https://doi.org/10.1038/srep10964*

- Together Platform (2023). Randstad case study: Skyrocketing retention rates by connecting employees with mentors. Retrieved from *https://www.togetherplatform.com/case-studies/randstad*

- Spotify Newsroom. (2022, December 20). 4 years of Heart & Soul: Mental health support at Spotify. Retrieved from *https://newsroom.spotify.com/2022-12-20/4-years-of-heart-soul-mental-health-support-at-spotify/*

- Spotify HR Blog. (2022, August 16). Mental health for Spotifiers and beyond: Normalizing the conversation. Retrieved from *https://hrblog.spotify.com/2022/08/16/mental-health-for-spotifiers-and-beyond-normalising-the-conversation*

- Spotify HR Blog. (2020, October 10). Every day is mental health day. Retrieved from *https://hrblog.spotify.com/2020/10/10/every-day-is-mental-health-day*

➤ Spotify Life at Spotify. (2023). Equity & Impact Report 2023 [PDF]. Retrieved from *https://www.lifeatspotify.com/reports/Spotify-Equity-Impact-Report-2023.pdf*

➤ Spotify Life at Spotify. (2022). Under the Spotlight: Heart & Soul Report 2022 [PDF]. Retrieved from *https://www.lifeatspotify.com/reports/Heart-And-Soul-Under-The-Spotlight-Report-2022.pdf*

➤ Division of Research, Kaiser Permanente. (2023, November 22). Peer support program helps ease physician burnout. Look Inside KP. Retrieved from *https://lookinside.kaiserpermanente.org/peer-support-program-helps-ease-physician-burnout/*

➤ Tolins, M. L., Sax, D., Rana, J., & Kaiser Permanente Division of Research. (2023, November 1). Implementation and effectiveness of a physician-focused peer support program. PLOS ONE. Retrieved from *https://journals.plos.org/plosone/article?id=10.1371/journal.pone.*

➤ Healthcare Innovation Group. (2023, November 16). Study: Kaiser Permanente Peer Support Program reduced burnout. Healthcare Innovation. Retrieved from *https://www.hcinnovationgroup.com/clinical-it/physician-burnout/news/53078436/study-kaiser-permanente-peer-support-program-reduced-burnout*

➤ ICD Events (2025, January 29). Molly Tolins, MD - Founder and Regional Director, Peer Outreach Support Team Kaiser Permanente Northern California. ICD Events. Retrieved from *https://icdevents.com/speaker/molly-tolins-md/*

➤ The role of Digital Tools in Enhancing Employee Well-being. Retrieved from *https://vorecol.com/blogs/blog-the-role-of-digital-tools-in-enhancing-employee-wellbeing-a-study-of-recent-software-solutions-177445*

➤ Microsoft. (n.d.). Introducing Microsoft Viva Engage. Microsoft Learn. Retrieved from *https://learn.microsoft.com/en-us/viva/engage/overview*

➤ Microsoft. (n.d.). Introducing Microsoft Viva Insights. Microsoft Learn. Retrieved 21 February 2025 from *https://learn.microsoft.com/en-us/viva/insights/introduction*

➤ Johnson & Johnson Human Performance Institute. (2017). Johnson & Johnson Human Performance Institute launches Corporate Athlete®

Resilience program. Retrieved from *https://www.prnewswire.com/news-releases/johnson—johnson-human-performance-institute-launches-corporate-athlete-resilience-program-300444628.html*

➢ Johnson & Johnson. (2023). Employee health, safety & well-being. Retrieved from *https://healthforhumanityreport.jnj.com/2023/our-employees/employee-health-safety-well-being*

➢ Johnson & Johnson. (2024). Human Performance Institute expands portfolio of C-suite executive development and well-being programs. Retrieved from *https://www.jnj.com/media-center/press-releases/johnson-johnson-human-performance-institute-expands-portfolio-of-c-suite-executive-development-and-wellbeing-programs*

➢ Tufts University & Johnson & Johnson Health and Wellness Solutions. (2023). New findings show sustained improvement in employee quality of life 18 months after training. Retrieved from *https://www.jnj.com/media-center/press-releases/new-findings-show-sustained-improvement-in-employee-quality-of-life-18-months-after-training*

➢ Human Capital Leadership Institute (HCLI). (n.d.). *Is the Johnson & Johnson approach to well-being set to shake up Asia?* Retrieved from *https://hcli.org/is-the-johnson-johnson-approach-to-well-being-set-to-shake-up-asia/*

➢ Janssen Asia Pacific. (n.d.). *Healthy minds mean healthy workplaces.* Retrieved from *https://www.janssen.com/apac/healthy-minds-mean-healthy-workplaces*

➢ Tik, M., Sladky, R., Luft, C., & Windischberger, C. (2018). Dopamine-producing areas of the brain inspire creativity: Neural correlates of the Aha! moment. Human Brain Mapping. *https://doi.org/10.1002/hbm.24073*

➢ Frontiers in Psychology Editorial Team (2023). Cognitive flexibility and entrepreneurial creativity: Enhancing adaptability through innovative thinking. Frontiers in Psychology. *https://doi.org/10.3389/fpsyg.2023.1292797*

➢ Mars, Incorporated (2013). Make the Difference Awards: Celebrating innovation and collaboration. Retrieved from *https://www.mars.com/sustainability-plan/working-with-others*

➤ Singapore Airlines. (2019, January 29). *Singapore Airlines opens digital innovation lab in drive to be the world's leading digital airline.* Singapore Airlines. Retrieved from *https://www.singaporeair.com/en_UK/be/media-centre/press-release/article/?q=en_UK/2019/January-March/ne0119-190129*

➤ Singapore Airlines. (n.d.). *KrisLab.* Singapore Airlines. Retrieved from *https://krislab.singaporeair.com/en*

➤ Cisco (2024). Mastering skills with play: The fusion of gaming and learning in Black Belt gamification. Retrieved from *https://blogs.cisco.com/partner/mastering-skills-with-play-the-fusion-of-gaming-and-learning-in-black-belt-gamification*

➤ PsicoSmart (2023). The impact of gamification on employee engagement and retention in remote training programs. Retrieved from *https://psico-smart.com/en/blogs/blog-the-impact-of-gamification-on-employee-engagement-and-retention-in-remote-training-programs-161613*

➤ Novembre, G., & Iannetti, G. D. (2021). Interpersonal neural synchronization and its implications for team collaboration. Nature Reviews Neuroscience, 22(2), 123–135. *https://doi.org/10.1038/s41583-020-00438-4*

➤ Quanta Magazine. (2024). The social benefits of getting our brains in sync. Retrieved from *https://www.quantamagazine.org/the-social-benefits-of-getting-our-brains-in-sync-20240328/*

➤ 5 Reasons why Vision is Important in Leadership (2021). Retrieved from *https://noahibrahim.org/5-reasons-why-vision-is-important-in-leadership-2/*

➤ Office Snapshots (2012). Pixar headquarters and the legacy of Steve Jobs. Retrieved from *https://officesnapshots.com/2012/07/16/pixar-headquarters-and-the-legacy-of-steve-jobs/*

➤ Business Insider. (2015). Steve Jobs designing Pixar office. Retrieved from *https://www.businessinsider.com/steve-jobs-designing-pixar-office-2015-3*

➤ Tradeline, Inc. (2024). Planning the future of Mayo Clinic's translational research workplace. Retrieved from *https://www.tradelineinc.com/reports/2024-7/planning-future-mayo-clinics-translational-research-workplace*

➤ HDR, Inc. (2024). Mayo Clinic Anna-Maria and Stephen Kellen Building. Retrieved from *https://www.hdrinc.com/portfolio/mayo-clinic-anna-maria-and-stephen-kellen-building*

➤ Hindustan Unilever Limited (2023). Performance Highlights FY 2023-24: Digital Transformation. Retrieved from *https://hul-performance-highlights.hul.co.in/performance-highlights-fy-2023-2024/digital-transformation.html*

➤ Hindustan Unilever Limited (2024). Reimagine HUL: Our Journey to an Intelligent Enterprise. Retrieved from *https://www.hul.co.in/files/reimagine-hul-summary.pdf*

➤ PMI (2024). Integrated Report 2023: Driving innovation through collaboration. Retrieved from *https://www.pmi.com/resources/docs/default-source/ir2023-documents/pmi-integrated-report-2023.pdf*

➤ Procurement Leaders. (2023). PMI's approach to cross-functional collaboration in new product strategy. Retrieved from *https://procurementleaders.com/content/pmi-cross-functional-collaboration-new-product-strategy/*

➤ People Matters. (2024, September 27). How AI is shaping the employee experience at DBS. Retrieved from *https://www.peoplematters.in/article/employee-engagement/how-ai-is-shaping-the-employee-experience-at-dbs-42840*

➤ Chief of Staff Asia. (2023). Case in point: How DBS Bank personalizes career coaching and enhances mobility with AI. Retrieved from *https://chiefofstaff.asia/news-and-insights/case-in-point-how-dbs-bank-personalises-career-coaching-enhances-mobility-with-ai/*

➤ DBS Bank (2023). DBS' AI-powered digital transformation. Retrieved from *https://www.dbs.com/artificial-intelligence-machine-learning/artificial-intelligence/dbs-ai-powered-digital-transformation.html*

➤ DHL Group (2023). DHL Innovation Centers: Shaping the future of logistics. Retrieved from *https://group.dhl.com/en/media-relations/press-releases/2023/dhl-breaks-ground-on-cutting-edge-european-innovation-center-in-germany-prioritizing-holistic-sustainability.html*

➤ DHL Group (2023). Employee development and training initiatives. Retrieved from *https://group.dhl.com/en/sustainability/social/employee-development.html*

➤ People Matters (2023). DHL Express: A workplace built on innovation and collaboration. Retrieved from *https://www.peoplematters.in/article/leadership/dhl-express-a-workplace-built-on-innovation-and-collaboration-42840*

➤ Rosenkranz, J. A., Venheim, E. R., & Padival, M. (2010). Chronic stress and amygdala neuronal dysfunction. Neuroscience, 165(3), 803–813. *https://doi.org/10.1016/j.neuroscience.2009.10.007*

➤ Miller, E. K., & Cohen, J. D. (2001). An integrative theory of prefrontal cortex function. Annual Review of Neuroscience, 24, 167–202. *https://doi.org/10.1146/annurev.neuro.24.1.167*

➤ OKR Quickstart. (2024). Domino's: Transforming business strategy with OKRs. Retrieved from *https://okrquickstart.com/testimonials/dominos*

➤ QuestionPro (2024). Domino's Pizza customer experience: A customer-centric journey. Retrieved from *https://www.questionpro.com/blog/dominos-pizza-customer-experience/*

➤ TM Forum (2020). Celcom's data governance program lays the foundation for greater value. Retrieved from *https://inform.tmforum.org/research-and-analysis/case-studies/celcoms-data-governance-program-lays-foundation-for-greater-value*

➤ FutureCIO (2020). Celcom says data governance is key to its digital transformation. Retrieved from *https://futurecio.tech/celcom-says-data-governance-is-key-to-its-digital-transformation/*

➤ Mizuho Financial Group (2023). Integrated Report 2023. Retrieved from *https://www.mizuho-fg.co.jp/investors/financial/annual/data2303/pdf/data2303_all_browsing.pdf*

➤ Mizuho Financial Group. (2022). Enhancing Corporate Culture Transformation Structure. Retrieved from *https://www.mizuhogroup.com/news/2022/11/20221114_2release_eng.html*

➤ HolacracyOne (2023). Holacracy at Zappos: A case study in self-management. Retrieved from *https://www.holacracy.org/wp-content/uploads/2023/08/Holacracy-WhitePaper-v5.pdf*

➢ Scirp.org (2023). Adapting to change: Exploring Zappos' self-management structure. Retrieved from *https://www.scirp.org/pdf/me_2023032215115639.pdf*

➢ Azbil Corporation (2019). Essential Goals for the SDGs. Retrieved from *https://www.azbil.com/csr/sdgs/sdgs.html*

➢ Azbil Corporation (2023). Risk Management System. Retrieved from *https://www.azbil.com/csr/basic/management.html*

➢ Azbil Corporation (2023). Integrated Report 2023. Retrieved from *https://www.azbil.com/press/231012.html*

➢ People Manager. (2023, May 27). Hyundai Motor India has implemented a role-based organizational structure. Retrieved from *https://peoplemanager.co.in/hyundai-motor-india-has-implemented-a-role-based-organisational-structure/*

➢ Moneycontrol. (2023, September 20). Hyundai Motor India net profit jumps 62.3% to Rs. 4709.25 crore in FY23. Retrieved from *https://www.moneycontrol.com/news/business/earnings/hyundai-motor-india-net-profit-jumps-62-3-to-rs-4709-25-crore-in-fy23-11398941.html*

➢ Business Standard. (2024, January 1). Hyundai Motor India total sales grow by 9%, reaching 765,786 units in 2023. Retrieved from *https://www.business-standard.com/industry/auto/hyundai-motor-india-total-sales-grow-9-reach-765-786-units-in-2023-124010100357_1.html*

➢ Smart 360 Feedback (2024). The impact of artificial intelligence on 360-degree evaluation systems. Retrieved from *https://smart-360-feedback.com/blogs/blog-the-impact-of-artificial-intelligence-on-360degree-evaluation-systems-162010*

➢ Edmondson, A. C. (1999). Psychological safety and learning behavior in work teams. Administrative Science Quarterly, 44(2), 350–383. *https://doi.org/10.2307/2666999*

➢ NeuroLeadership Institute (2022). Psychological safety and accountability: Insights from Amy Edmondson. Retrieved from *https://neuroleadership.com/your-brain-at-work/psychological-safety-and-accountability-insights-from-amy-edmondson*

➢ Capgemini Research Institute (2023). Discussion with Amy Edmondson: Building a psychologically safe workplace. Retrieved from *https://www.capgemini.com/insights/research-library/discussion-with-amy-edmondson*

➤ Bonnstetter, R. J., & Bonnstetter, B. J. (2021). Brain activation imaging in emotional decision-making and accountability systems: Implications for leadership development. Journal of Cognitive Neuroscience, 33(5), 729–738. *https://doi.org/10.1177/1550059420916636*

➤ Awan, S. H., Habib, N., & Ahmed, A. (2020). Effectiveness of performance management systems for employee engagement: The role of clarity and feedback mechanisms. SAGE Open, 10(2), 2158244020969383. *https://doi.org/10.1177/2158244020969383*

➤ ODRL (2019). The history of 360-degree feedback. Retrieved from *https://www.odrl.org/2019/12/27/360-degree-feedback-history/*

➤ MetLife (2023). Sustainability Report 2023. Retrieved from *https://sustainabilityreport.metlife.com/report/*

➤ Harver (2024). MetLife's HR Heroes: Proving the benefits of employee engagement. Retrieved from *https://www.harver.com/blog/metlife-hr-heroes-proves-benefits-of-employee-engagement/*

➤ MetLife (2024, April 4). MetLife named to Fortune Magazine's 2024 list of the 100 best companies to work for. Retrieved from *https://www.metlife.com/about-us/newsroom/2024/april/metlife-named-to-fortune-magazines-2024-list-of-the-100-best-companies-to-work-for/*

➤ Business Insider (2016). IBM now uses the ACE app to give and receive real-time feedback. Retrieved from *https://www.businessinsider.com/ibm-now-uses-the-ace-app-to-give-and-receive-real-time-feedback-2016-5*

➤ ICMR India (2003). The Taj's People Philosophy and STAR System. Retrieved from *https://www.icmrindia.org/free%20resources/casestudies/The%20Tajs%20People%20Philosophy-Case.htm*

➤ Deshpande, R. (2011). Terror at the Taj Bombay: Customer-Centric Leadership. Harvard Business School Case Study. Retrieved from *https://www.hbs.edu/faculty/Pages/item.aspx?num=40223*

➤ Unstop (2025). The Taj Group: Valuing employees as assets through the Taj People Philosophy and STAR System. Retrieved from *https://unstop.*

➤ com/blog/the-taj-group-valuing-employees-as-assets-through-the-taj-people-philosophy-and-the-star-system

➤ BHP (2017). BHP Operating System (BOS): Driving operational excellence. Retrieved from *https://www.bhp.com/-/media/documents/media/reports-and-presentations/2017/171018_bhpoperationalreviewforthequarterended30september2017.pdf*

➤ Australian Resources & Investment. (2022). How BHP beats the cost crunch. Retrieved from *https://www.australianresourcesandinvestment.com.au/2022/07/06/how-bhp-beats-the-cost-crunch/*

➤ BHP (2024). Engagement and Perception Surveys: Employee insights for growth. Retrieved from *https://www.bhp.com/sustainability/people*

➤ FlexCareers (2024). We're working hard to close the pay gap. Retrieved from *https://www.flexcareers.com.au/employers/bhp/articles/we-re-working-hard-to-close-the-pay-gap*

➤ UN Global Compact (2022). BHP Group Limited – Communication on Progress FY22. Retrieved from *https://unglobalcompact.org/participation/report/cop/advanced/477153*

www.ingramcontent.com/pod-product-compliance
Lightning Source LLC
Chambersburg PA
CBHW031119130726
47988CB00006B/2141